Painting: some basic principles

Cover
Miró: Cartoon for Tapestry, 'Personnages Rythmiques', 1934
Kunstsammlung Nordrhein-Westfalen, Düsseldorf
© *Association pour la diffusion des Arts Graphiques et Plastiques, Paris 1965*
Photo: John Webb, Brompton Studios

Magritte: 'Golconde'. Honour to the poets of the commonplace!
Magritte and Léger have faced both the appearance and sensation of the
twentieth century. Technically Magritte is on common ground with
the movie. But where the cinema needs a succession of shots, the painting
presents simultaneous images on which we can privately dwell.

Painting: some basic principles

Frederick Gore

Studio Vista: London
Reinhold Publishing Corporation: New York

A Studio Vista/Reinhold Art Paperback edited by John Lewis

SET IN 9/12 GARAMOND

PRINTED IN THE NETHERLANDS

BY N.V. DRUKKERIJ KOCH & KNUTTEL, GOUDA

Contents

When we talk about painting, we are not discussing one pure unmixed form of art. We are generalizing about a variety of activities differing widely in technique and aesthetic purpose. We lump them together under one name because they are similar: technical similarities begin with the use of pigment on a surface, aesthetic similarities with the intention to make meaningful images which are projections of visual experience (real or invented). Ikons, frescoes, cabinet painting, miniatures, watercolours or action paintings are very different forms, but we class them all as 'painting'. There are a host of other art forms associated with painting – mosiac, stained glass, tapestry, carpet design, painted pottery and tiles, enamel work and prints – which insofar as they approach the same expressive purposes as painting and condense experience to a surface image in two dimensions can be identified with painting. Obviously there is a special complementary relationship between painting and sculpture. They both deal with the same matter – images which result from visual and tactile perception – but technically they are entirely different. Sculpture is 'in the round', painting 'on the flat'. But painting has borrowed heavily from sculpture (especially in its most representative forms); relief sculpture can be almost indistinguishable from painting, and there are art forms which lie between the two.

The truth is that there is no such thing as 'pure' art. We may divide the arts into architecture, music, dance, sculpture, painting, drama, poetry and so on, but these distinctions have arisen by custom and convenience as part of an historical process. In every age new techniques have been invented, old forms forgotten, still older ones revived, new and old combined. Art forms are continually changing. There is nothing absolute about their nature. Since Leonardo endeavoured to raise painting to the level of 'fine' art, the accredited list has changed; some arts have been absorbed by science (mathematics), some are no longer mentionable (rhetoric), others have been devalued (oratory to public speaking). As society changes ancient and primitive crafts lose caste (tatooing), go underground (divination), become children's games, or like those of the armourer and the swordsmith are embalmed in

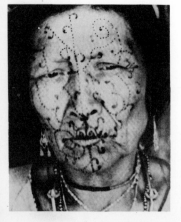

The painted face of a Caduveo woman. Photograph by Claude Lévi-Strauss

6

Pol Bury: 'Aluminio', 1963

Takis: 'Télélumière', 1964

ceremonial. Architecture, music, drama, painting, sculpture, poetry are not constants. The list of accepted arts will change again. The great smiths, charismatic figures in history and legend, have turned into engineers, equally awesome as the faceless sculptors of a machine age. The architect, hardly established in a separate profession, turns from building to town planning, and as the roads spread out may have to landscape our total topographical environment, to become a new creature half sociologist, half engineer. Young painters gradually arming themselves with new materials and scientific knowledge restlessly and aggressively search for new forms, not as in the years of futurism, cubism and surrealism in order to produce an art in sympathy with a new scientific age, but with a consciousness of power, aware that their aesthetic inventions discharged into industry and mass media (and fed back into art again) could change the environment and mould the scientific culture to which they are already tuned. But what they do may no longer fall into the cosy categories of painting and sculpture. Environmental art, constructivism, pop art, kinetic art, auto-destructive art are pointers.

Some people consider opera to be an indigestible mixture of music and drama. Yet the combination of song and dance and spoken word seems to go back into the remotest origins of the theatre. Drama, initially words and gestures (mime), has also embraced music, dancing, costume, make-up, lighting, scene painting, stage engineering, theatre architecture, masks, puppets and heaven knows what besides. Mystery plays offered the mediaeval painter direct visual contact with his religious subject matter and the masques and carnivals on the streets of Florence or waterways of Venice gave the Italian painter the power to paint pagan scenes with the same tender and affectionate immediacy.

Hokusai painting his gigantic bird before a vast audience with a broom dipped in indian ink, surrealist high jinks (Dali in a diving suit), Matthieu jousting with his canvas, or present day 'happenings' are part of the urge that painting has towards the theatre. Diaghileff had an effective influence on modern design because of the opportunities which he gave to Picasso, Derain, Laurencin and the rest to work for the theatre in the Russian tradition of scene painting on the floor. It was here they learnt to compose in the flat.

Photography developed from painting and inevitably led to the motion picture and a return to drama in a new form with the dramatic action developed visually as much as or more than in words. If the cinema and television outpace the legitimate theatre for a century it

7

will be parallel to the ascendancy of the mosaic over painting and sculpture in Byzantium. Both Pericles and Cicero would have been surprised if they had been told that the technique for decorating bathroom floors was to develop into a great art, a vehicle for deep emotion and profound religious concepts, a visible theology. In its classical form, tenth-century mosaic combined the essential characteristics of sculpture, painting and drama, ordered architecturally.

The renewal of art is by mixture. New materials, techniques and ideas lead into the unknown land between fixed stockades of academies, historians and schools: art forms which appear pure are often dead. All art forms are hybrid. There is no separation between the arts but an infinite (existing or potential) variety of art forms which use a selection of means from a common pool. The means develop from the factors of sense perception: visual, tactile, auditory, vocal – the movements of the body; rhythms, pulsation, balance – combined with such materials as wood, plaster, pigments and metals. (Perhaps I should say olfactory too: perfumery, tea blending or cooking are surely arts. Claude Lorraine is reported to have declared there were only two arts: painting and ornamental pastry.) The grading of fine art and applied art, folk art, industrial art, domestic art is nonsense (although a colloquial convenience). Yesterday's industrial or domestic art is tomorrow's fine art.

David Hockney: 'Portable Mirror'

The older patterns of industry become folk art, just as popular tunes do when their composers are forgotten. Certainly fine art must mean art which has outstripped its utilitarian purpose and which communicates as well as decorates. But many applied arts have had their turn as fine art – pottery in China, tapestry in the Middle Ages, carpets in Persia. For desert nomads in lands where Mahommedan iconoclasm in any case forbade figurative images, woven tent hangings and carpets provided decoration. These became fine art because their imaginative significance transcended decoration, and yet they remained folk art since they were woven to the composition of an itinerant pattern caller, from thread dyed by the tribal wise woman, by children (after twelve the girls were said to be distracted too easily by adult interest). Fine art is not necessarily an act of individual genius.

The sounds of music take their significance from the cadences of the voice – in lamentation, joy, love, incantation, aggression: the link is with speech and mime, while the rhythms of music are shared by the dance. Similarly at their simplest the technical ingredients of painting are line, shared with calligraphy, and colour, shared especially with applied arts – tapestry, ceramics, textiles, stained glass, jewellery and so on. Using different ranges of pigment, these arts often explored colour for its own sake beyond the possibilities of painting. Extension of the various formal means towards tactile realism came with the imitation of sculpture – modelling, balance, weight and movement of mass. The necessary influence of architecture on wall painting extended the concepts of structural relationships and the theories of composition (the mathematical elements of proportion, scale, perspective). There is no need to enlarge on the storytelling aspect of painting and the common ground with literature – especially interesting is the picture in relation to the manuscript and the printed page – or the closeness of painting to drama; the interchange between them leads back through history to forgotten rituals. The analogy between colour and music has been a twentieth-century preoccupation. Painting has always been an art as mixed as the cinema or mosaic.

In a social context, we may say that painting is the child of architecture (the formal) but also of drama (the expressive). These are the public arts, the arts of society. Man acts and man makes. Among his actions are birth, love, hunting, sowing, war and death. He makes his dwelling places and his tools: the attempt to understand his actions and the forces which cause them result in drama. The realization of himself as a builder results in architecture.

Painting embraces both acting and making – the dramatic and the architectonic, the expressive and the formal – it is wrong to consider one as content and the other as form. Equally it is false to equate one with romantic tendencies, the other with classical. (This is an antiquated literary distinction.) The mimetic and expressive side of painting is allied to literature, and is none the worse for it. But it was an accident of history that the final phases of extreme naturalism were associated with romantic tendencies in literature. The swing to abstraction is not a movement of the pendulum from dramatic to formal or romantic to classical. The dialectical conflict between dramatic and architectural, expressive and formal, remains in abstract painting as much as it does in all kinds of painting.

In drama the conflict is first between man and the forces outside man (natural forces, deities), then the conflict between men themselves, and finally the conflict within man. Painting also has been concerned with the relationship of man to his environment.

But the conflict in modern terms is not the physical conflict between man and nature, but that between psychological forces within man and

'The Empress Theodora'. Mosaic at S. Vitale, Ravenna.

the forces of environment, which are both physical and psychological. The literal description of man's physical appearance and of the objects which surround him can now be omitted. The conflict is no longer between moral order and natural order (between spiritual and physical) since man is no longer considered partly divine, but a being inseparable from his environment. His interior world and the exterior world are seen as facets of the same order (and the same chaos). Painting has become concerned with the interior landscape (which is a part of man) as much as the exterior (of which man is part). The subject of painting is a state of mind. The difference between figurative and abstract painting is in the degree to which the appearance of objects is retained or eliminated. The extent to which they should describe objects and the way in which they should describe them has become the special problem of all painters.

A good deal is known about the mechanism of the eye, something about how the brain receives and interprets the messages which arrive through the eye, almost nothing about the psychological processes involved in the act of seeing. How do we recognize things? Do we hold in our minds filing cabinets of visual memory traces with which to compare each new experience? Do we store away complete images? The way in which some visual memories spring fully armed and clothed from our heads would suggest so. How individualistic is our vision? Are there images of an archetypal kind, common to all men, or simply accretions of personal experience, so that people who have led very different lives may see things very differently? How is our sight connected with our other senses – touch, taste, smell and hearing – or related to our ability to balance and move, to our muscular activities. So little is known of all this that all but the simplest aesthetic theories must for the present remain fanciful or intuitive.

It may also be true that not only can we never know exactly how other ages have thought about what they saw and what they painted, but that they actually saw quite differently from ourselves. Speed of movement from early childhood may be altering our way of seeing things, as well as our way of thinking about what we see. As well as this acceleration of movement in ourselves and the things round us, an increased range of appearances from the air, under water, or through cameras, microscopes, telescopes, television, extended knowledge of physical and biological patterns which correspond to visual and tactile experience even though we cannot see them, the consciousness of our existence in four dimensions are all altering the psychological background to vision and even the actual machinery of perception.

We have blind spots in our appreciation of the past. Allegorical symbolism in Renaissance art means very little now; we blithely ignore it and look for some other meaning without asking to what extent allegory influenced vision. Yet we probably admit that the eye sees what the mind is seeking; men will depict the same objects quite differently because they see them in relation to a different order of reality. Physical appearances are not absolute. If we agree that the piety and simple faith of a mediaeval artist coloured his vision, why suppose that the Egyptians did not see in a way which is similar to the conventions in which they worked. The most honourable way of treating our ancestors is to give them the benefit of the doubt and assume that they painted in a certain way not from ignorance but because they saw in that way. The fact is that we treat, as if it was arbitrary artistic convention, the evidence that different ages have had different modes of thought and therefore ways of seeing.

The problems of modern painting (and the fact that painters seem to be conscious of treating painting as a problem) are caused not by the attempt to find a new kind of painting, but to come to terms with the new and changing ways in which we already see. In this new climate the stumbling block of most art criticism is the mimetic element in painting. Almost daily we read remarks which imply that from the early Renaissance until the invention of the camera painters were busy attempting to imitate nature. The literal imitation of appearances for its own sake has never at any time been the aim of respectable painting: every painter knows that if he uses certain means to make his work more like in any one respect, it will be less like in some other respect. Painters are concerned with ideas, not with an anecdotal inventory of visual details. Philistine adults pretend what every child knows to be untrue, that appearances can be copied, confusing art with nature. Only a tree can look like a tree. If we could sit down with paint and brushes and paint a full copy of a tree, we would produce a tree, not a painting of a tree. It only takes a few false starts at painting to discover that this is impossible. At this point someone will say: 'What about photography?' But we can only photograph some aspect of a tree, its shape in silhouette or the detail of tangled leaves and branches, or contrast of light and shade, or depth and richness of texture. Even with a camera we cannot make a tree.

The more representative of some truth in nature that a painter (or photographer) wishes his work to be, the more selective he must be

'S. Francis supporting the Lateran Basilica', detail, Church of S. Francis, Assisi

and the less can he literally copy nature.

Everybody who goes to the theatre knows that an actor does not behave on the stage as people do in life. His interpretation of behaviour may be more or less realistic, but it must be an interpretation through the medium of his art. It must be modified to suit the form of theatre; performance to a vast amphitheatre requires big and slow gestures, but even in the most intimate realistic theatre the audience will want to hear and that is not like life. In any case he must select, simplify, exaggerate; in tragedy and in comedy his emphasis and his timing will be different. Detailed study of actual behaviour may be the key to character, but distortion gives significance.

Art is not life but the interpretation of life. A haphazard stringing together of detailed observations is meaningless in the theatre, and equally meaningless in painting.

Meaningless at the other extreme of theatre or painting are formal gestures and abstract patterns, unless they represent a logical development of ideas and emotions: abstract art in seeking direct intuitive contact with reality uses hidden patterns of thought that have been distilled from naturalistic sources. This is not to say that abstract painters extract their motifs from visual experience. But the power of the imagination to give meaning to forms symbolically and by association derives from the ability of primitive man to identify himself with his environment and to act out the drama of his own existence in rituals – mime, song, drawing, carving. These cathartic acts which assuaged his fears, hungers and joys demanded the imitation of natural forces: animals, crops, earth, water, fire, weapons, enemies, gods, fecundity. Shapes, colours and lines only take on meaning in the light of man's ability to mime. The child, too, at the age when he is most disturbed by the struggle to come to terms with his environment, acts out his anxieties and desires in his drawing. His explorations of physical reality are coloured by the phantasies which are his understanding of reality and his attempt to dominate circumstances. His observations and his formal inventions are indistinguishable. Primitive men and children make the mark and see it as a sign. They make the sign and it becomes a hallowed mark. Representation and ritual gesture are identified. The unconscious and the nameless are secretly named.

If some forms of painting draw most from external observation and others from the intrinsic behaviour of shapes, lines and colours, these two extremes are complementary and necessary to each other. Not only is modern abstract art made intelligible by the glimpses which

Toulouse-Lautrec: 'The Bed'.
Interpretation, not imitation

Louvre, Paris

we get from primitive and child art of the concealed springs of meaning, but also we read these non-figurative paintings in relation to the figurative paintings which preceded them and to which they overtly relate: in space through colour to Cézanne, in the organization of planes to cubism, in gesture and handwriting to Van Gogh, in localization of colour to Gauguin (and through these to Rubens, Poussin and a continuous tradition). The forms of art have their meaning in the context of the culture of which they are a part. Non-figurative art exists in the context of figurative art.

Similarly the meaning of a figurative work of art lies in its abstract organization: both in the effect of the ingredients separately and in combination, both for conveying their own meaning and at the same time the representational meaning. By this I mean that we can read the work piecemeal, enjoying pieces of colour or line or shape for their own sake and attaching customary (or our own subjective) significance to them; we also see the work as a whole and its qualities of organization and design, so that various relationships take on significance, and at the same time (or alternatively) we are digesting the figurative matter contained in the picture, and the story or ideas which it conveys. These are not different activities, but the same interrogation of the same shapes and lines and colours at different levels of experience. There is not one significance for the 'form' and another for the 'subject'. A red is a cap; it is also a note of violence; it is also a complement to the greys which it enlivens; it also marks a place in space, establishes the position of a figure – it could not do one of these things without doing the other. Of course there are many imperfections and discrepancies in paintings, but there is only one language; and in this language the fact of a red or a straight line or a curve comes first, the composition and the configuration come together, but the representational meaning is contained in the whole meaning – the meaning at different levels which are produced by the formal means and give to the painting its correspondence to life. Paintings are open to personal interpretation, but the painter makes clear his intention in his design. Whether abstract or figurative, precise design limits the possibilities of personal interpretation. Even the most naturalistic painting is not simply a conglomeration of recognizable objects, and composition is not simply a way of fitting together recognizable objects to imitate an event or a scene so that it can be read and understood comfortably. Nature is contradictory (we cannot, for instance, give full value to the contrast of dark and light and also to differences of colour – we cannot even see them at the same time). Choice must be made, 'nature' must be ordered. Ordered according to what? An idea of what 'nature' is? A story we wish to tell? An emotion we feel? From the answer stems the sort of work which we are to produce; the different 'schools' of painting. But whatever way we paint we are committed to an abstract activity. It is then the total of interacting lines and shapes and colours, of planes and rhythms, of plain and patterned areas, of mass and weight and movement, of space and solid, which make manifest at one and the same time the visible drama and the thoughts and emotions which lie behind – the overriding idea which gives coherence. The forms in painting cannot be copied from nature, but must be equivalents to nature, plastic signs and images built up from simple formal ingredients which both separately and together have intrinsic meaning – that is the meaning of red or black, curve or straight, smooth or rough, of swift movement or slow, dark or light – and which, while they indicate events, are also composed musically.

The work of art is the creation of the spectator as well as the artist. The representational meaning is contained by and gains profundity from a wider imaginative connotation. This may be an intellectual field (as in some religious and allegorical or didactic art, and in portraiture) or emotional, but is presented in a plastic and concrete form which allows the spectator to contribute his own thoughts, his own ideas, emotions, associations and latent imagery. Even in the most didactic art form there must be scope for the spectator to attach his sympathy and share in the process of creation. Far from wishing everybody to interpret his painting in the same way, the painter hopes that each will see something different.

Of course the history of painting is the history of how men have looked and seen, and the camera developed from painting as a product of their desire for optical realism. But obviously it is not true that art until this century mainly evolved towards ever better camera-like recordings of the visible world, or that the camera ousted realistic painting: it is the nature of realism which has changed with the development of science, of which the camera is only a small part. Obviously even the least of the masters of naturalism aimed to understand and compose, not to record. They were concerned with the meaning of the visible world, and their paintings are interrogations of the visible in order to come to terms with reality. Of course painters have always tried to increase the store of visual data, the raw material of their craft. But it would be fatuous to see the science with which Michelangelo or Tintoretto were able to compose magisterially with human bodies moving in space as endeavours to record appearances more accurately. No one could ever suppose that the 'Last Judgment' (or any single figure in the Sistine Chapel) looks like a slice of visible life or that Tintoretto's 'Last Supper' corresponds to common experience. 'St Francis feeding the birds', although less naturalistic technically, has a dramatic simplicity much nearer to what we actually see. To an honest modern eye those armoured figures bashing each other with sword and battle axe in Uccello's 'Rout of San Romano' have a dynamic truth and a more literal presence than the gracious ballets of Raphael. What we accept

Uccello: 'The Rout of S. Romano'
detail

National Gallery, London

as natural is subject to fashion. But it is clear that the Italians sought the power to manipulate appearances and not to record them.

Certainly the detailed recording of household chattels was what Dutch painters were paid to do and loved to do: the age paid homage to domestic gods. Pots and pans and food and houses and clothes and carpets could not be handled too closely or lovingly with the eyes. With the aid of mirrors, lenses and measuring instruments, they sought an intense optical realism which even the camera has not surpassed. Scientific practicality which had provided Holland with improved

Vermeer: 'Lady seated at the Virginals'

forms of industrial power (windmills and watermills), land drainage and reclamation, and supported many mercantile skills from accountancy to shipbuilding, and also disinterested scientific enquiry of the kind which developed the lens, are both deployed in Dutch painting. But the passion for unblinkered truth was also a consequence of the moral climate of Protestantism. The paintings of Vermeer are models of scientific analysis as well as practical engineering. But their mathematical serenity and domestic harmony are the result of a structural clarity which also holds suspended conflicts between piety and free enquiry, mercantilism and moral purpose, luxury and frugality, discipline and freedom, and conceals the seeds of doubt inherent in capitalism and democracy. The natural comparison is with Piero della Francesca, that other mathematician of external calm and interior crisis. The pursuit of optical accuracy was part of a deeper purpose.

Naturalism is conventional: highly naturalistic techniques combine a variety of conventions into one complicated web: unity is easily lost and like an elaborate card castle the illusion collapses (to laughter). Paintings which appear most natural are often those which use few and simple conventions of a very artificial but easily accepted kind. Conventions are subject to fashion; what seems natural to one generation seems naïve to another and sometimes virtually incomprehensible.

Art is illusion, not in the sense of optical illusions but in the sense that the theatre sustains an illusion. By accepting certain glaring artificialities (conventions), we are transported into a world which is consistent with itself, and commands belief. It is consistency and correspondence to reality which causes us to accept conventions. For a work of art is not reality: it is a *model of reality*. It is a play on reality. It is a toy. We are able to play with it: we are able to play round it with ideas; we come to understand it, and through it to understand reality. This is necessary because we cannot by a direct approach understand reality. A work of art is convincing to the degree that it is a *model of reality* and that our ideas can play round it *as if it were reality*.

If a work of art such as a play contains ideas, it takes the form of a conflict of ideas; an argument in itself is not a work of art until it is presented in a concrete form as a conflict. A work of art must embody ideas in a coherent and concrete form in the physical medium of drama, or painting, or music. The 'word' must be made 'flesh'. In drama the argument must be presented as a conflict of ideas contained by the interaction of personalities and events. The artist does not present his ideas; he presents a model of reality which contains ideas and to which his audience can attach their ideas, participating. Similarly a painting may contain ideas figuratively or in an abstract way, but a model of reality need not be made in terms of intellectual ideas. Ideas are not reality but about reality. Valid ideas are models of reality but not necessarily works of art. Works of art are concrete models made manifest in a physical substance. Painting is concerned with sensory experience and the model provided by painting is a visual model of reality, an image about which we can have ideas, emotions, associations, and which in itself may contain or imply possible ideas, emotions and associations. But a conflict will also be implied – the dramatic presentation of alternatives.

If the work of art which is a model of reality were reality, we could not understand it: the play of ideas and therefore understanding is conditional on alternatives. We can only understand a situation by comparing it with alternatives. Reality is either *becoming*, in which case we are chained to time and space and the alternatives are all in the future, which we cannot know; or it is *being*, in which case there are no alternatives since a thing which is cannot be other than it is. Alternatives can only be seen in models and in the ideas which are attached to them. In plain words, the closer to reality we are the less we can see: we cannot face an art form which is too like life (tragedy which is too realistic, painting which pretends too great a realism). In the same degree as art approaches to reality the harder it becomes to see it as reality and to see any meaning in it.

The conventions of art must be sufficiently artificial or they will not convince. A condition of art is that it should allow us to consider the possibility of things being other than they are (as well as what they are). Phantasy is the criticism of reality, before it is an escape from it. It is only in detachment that reality can be discussed.

Excessive naturalism tends to produce absurdity, while abstraction out of contact with visual experience leads from painting to one of the other arts – literature. The conventions of painting must be appropriate to coloured images on a flat surface. The flat surface provides the essential artificiality which separates painting from life, and it must always be respected.

On the other hand, because we live in three dimensions and the things which we wish to discuss derive from the experience of three dimensions, painters have always been particularly preoccupied with space – the problem of representing three dimensions on a simple surface. Because we move in time, they have also been preoccupied with movement. Different ages and artists have found different solutions, but it is clear that the relationship between the painting and what it represents (whether a physical event or a psychological state) is symbolic. We grow used to old conventions, and the difficulty (which we all have to some degree) in appreciating the new in art is that it never seems to be quite painting (or sculpture or music) but something else. It appears to break the rules. The first stage in understanding is to kick away preconceptions – the mystique of oil painting (or fresco or watercolour), the sanctity of tonal painting or the masterliness of thick paint (or thin). If the form of painting is changing then so are the rules. The second stage, unnecessary for enjoyment but necessary for full understanding, is to learn something of the principles which are necessary to all forms of painting, and some of the ways in which these are extended and modified by different materials and techniques and intentions to produce the conventions which characterize the work of different painters in different ages and places.

Tintoretto: 'Susannah and the Elders'

Kunsthistorisches Museum, Vienna

Flat colour   Ikon of Saint George from Novgorod

Each area of this ikon has its own local colour which denotes a separate object. The background of sky is red, the horse is white, the body of the dragon grey-blue, and so on down to each detail. Colour and shape correspond exactly so that the colour makes the shapes which identify each object. But these coloured shapes also combine to make the design of the painting. The pattern of the design is very obvious – there is no sign of art to conceal art – it might even seem too obvious to someone brought up on Raphael or Corot, but this method of composition with areas of local colour has one tremendous strength: the means which identify the objects and therefore tell the story, and the design which gives the painting its aesthetic appeal, are one and the same and absolutely inseparable. This formula demands a most rigorous discipline and great talent – any weakness or uncertainty in the design and any failure in the formal patterns to promote the action of the story are instantly revealed. This is an act of faith which requires an iron nerve – the courage which goes with simplicity and a pure heart. It is not surprising to learn that a life of holiness was the rule for the painter monks, to ensure images which were holy, or that they were supported by a learned and hallowed tradition. Such technical mastery in utter simplicity of means belongs to religious art and firm tradition.

Lines and movement

A black line bounds not all but most of the shapes. (The contrast of a black line with the white of the horse would have been too strong.) The composition is concerned with balance and with movement. Movement comes from the incredible arabesque of the springing line. Architectural balance and dramatic movement are dialectal polarities in composition – the necessary conflict which contains life. The painter has a classical concern with movement held in suspense. But this line also makes the horse and rider alive.

Balance and symmetry

It is the Saint's head which must command reverence. Therefore, by its central position and because it is cutting the frame, the head is held in suspense; the pale aureole relates it as the still apex of a pyramid to the white springing shape of the horse. But the axis of the head is parallel to the axis of the horse's body and also echoes the diagonal movement of the horse. Note the small and larger curves which echo the halo – the horse's neck, the coiled body of the dragon. The spear counters, by its diagonal, the diagonal of the axis of the horse. Moving down from the head there is an offset balance on each side of the body: between cloak and horse's neck, back from horse's neck to horse's hind quarters, and from hind quarters across to the front of the dragon. At the same time there is a symmetrical balance in the lower part of the picture. On the right dragon's head echoes horse's head. On the left the shape of the cave is an exact counterpart to the horse's hind quarters. The horse's tail and the dragon's tail echo each other, and close the arabesque on this side, while the dragon's head meets the horse's hooves on the other.

The spaces left out

The splendid balance and nicely calculated proportion of the three red spaces left between! Most masterly touch of all – the red space under the belly lifts the horse into the air. This left-out space is also the pivot of the whole composition. Remove it with your hand and all the drawing becomes more ordinary. It is this area which gives a shock of movement and of truth to the whole painting. Here the straight line of the belly joins the two mountains and divides the upper half of the painting from the lower – Heaven from earth, the Saint from the dragon. A perspective (and therefore our position as spectators) is economically stated. The head of the Saint is looking down at us and we see the under-side of his cloak. So we find our place a little above the miserable dragon: by this machinery the Saint rides over all triumphant.

Naturalism 'The Baptism in the Jordan by Piero Della Francesca (p. 24)'

The expression 'naturalism' is used in more than one sense. In an historical sense it means the kind of painting that was developed by those painters of the early Renaissance who first began to enquire into the actual nature of physical reality. It is sometimes said that they presupposed the development of science. Indeed if we look at Piero della Francesca's 'Baptism' in the National Gallery it is very easy to see in him the duality of modern man which is behind each moral crisis which we face. On the one hand he adheres to strictly Byzantine iconography – how else would he safeguard the historic truth of the story which he tells, how else retain the sense that there is a spiritual

Ikon of S. George, Novgorod School, late fourteenth century

Russian Museum, Leningrad

Piero della Francesca: 'The Baptism in the Jordan'

National Gallery, London

'Baptism'. Mosaic at Daphni Catholicon, Athens

'Baptism'. Details of mosaic at S. Mark's, Venice

existence behind the visible? If we compare this painting with a Byzantine Baptism (see left), we see that he has not only been at great pains to keep to the traditional iconography but that there is a suggestion of affection for the unknown original which he followed. Not only are the figures placed in their conventional places and attitudes, but Christ's head cuts the skyline symbolically between the hills, the mysterious foliage of the big tree replaces the circle from which God the Father usually extends His hand in blessing, the shape of an axe is echoed by the Byzantine hat of the priestly figure in the background, and, most curious of all, Christ's loincloth has taken over the motif of the waves which would flow across the lower part of his body in the Byzantine original. The painting has the domed shape of a mosaic in a niche and the illusion of curved space.

On the other hand, while he almost copies, Piero also aimed at extraordinary realism. The way in which he treats each object in the painting asserts that the physical universe can be discussed fully in purely physical terms: God is no longer necessary for its existence. The equilibrium of a standing figure has never been studied with more passionate interest. Christ's legs and feet are human legs and feet explored anatomically for their structural beauty; the way they support the weight of the body down to the ground is the positive statement of an observed natural law; and the ground sustains their weight by an equal and opposite force. The stream winds away and the ground is flattened in accordance with an optical perspective, while the reflections of the bright figures beyond the man undressing convey a visual sensation astonishingly like that of a painter who is working on the spot.

We see in this painting physical relationships explored with the passion of a new discovery. It seems natural that painters, less suspect of heresy in their manual craft, and at a time when writers were fully engaged in translating and learning the rediscovered classics, using their eyes frankly and then asking what lay behind appearances, should first start that logical enquiry into the nature of things which was to become scientific. Perspective, tender modelling and atmosphere contribute to the sensation that everything in the painting has its precise position in space in relation to every other part.

Perhaps more than any other in the National Gallery, this painting shows the principle sought and later established in European painting, that relationships of space by means of line, shape and colour working together should achieve an ordered whole. Continuous spatial relationships are stated equally by values of colour and by the mathematical organization of volumes, so that the painting, while still affirming faith in God's purpose, comes to be a microcosm, the model of a finite material universe.

Since then it has rarely been possible for a European painter, however abstract, to use relationships of shape or colour without the consciousness that either they correspond to a reality which is physical or that he is reacting against this. I do not mean, for example, that a colour scheme corresponds to anything physically recognizable, but that it retains a sense of structure as opposed to colour which is purely symbolic, which we might dub literary, or that it is simply surface pattern unrelated to volume, which we might call decorative.

The strong structural and architectonic element in European painting was inherited from both classical and Byzantine art – but it is the relating of all the ingredients of the painting to a measurable space which is characteristic of naturalism and became a permanent influence in Western art.

It is clear that naturalism in this historical sense means a conceptual form of art primarily concerned not with appearances but with the actual physical nature of the thing seen. This may involve the artist in symbolic rendering of things which cannot necessarily be seen, but which are essential to his enquiry. Appearances are used as a means to establish the actual nature of the object seen.

Obviously there is another use of the expression to mean paintings which in some respects look extremely like their subject matter. Unfortunately things in painting which at first appear to be very like something are often not; a horse appears to be extraordinarily like a horse till we question if it could ever run. An important point has to be made here. Logically there is no reason why the formal ingredients of a painting should be interdependent to the extent of representing a complete unity of physical space. This is a tradition which might now be ignored, but it is worth telling anyone who intends to abandon it that it is this traditional completeness which has made possible the idea of the work of art as an end in itself. Wall paintings of Egypt, African and Mexican art, carvings on Indian temples, Persian miniatures, Byzantine decorations – all these and many more served a religious, illustrative, instructional, or some other social purpose. The idea of a work of art as an object of contemplation with the right to serve no purpose of instruction or propaganda is tied to the idea of the complete and self-sufficient microcosm.

Egyptian painting,
c. 1400 B.C.
British Museum, London

Chapter III   Drawing

All the arts share a common pool of formal means which correspond to our perceptual responses. Each art makes use of these in different materials. First there is movement. We know the world because we move; we know ourselves because we move. I move, therefore I am. The connection between the movement within (which is myself) and the movement outside is touch. I touch, therefore the world exists. The refined instruments of touch are the ear, the eye and the hand. Movement heard, movement seen, movement felt, all are equally subject to such mathematical partition as interval, quantity, proportion, symmetry and asymmetry, by which we relate the movement within us to the movements outside and distinguish their changing patterns.

In painting we are concerned with sight and touch. The eye discerns colours, the hand explores surfaces. From areas of colours and their boundaries we obtain shapes and lines. From the surfaces which we feel we obtain flat planes and curves, sharpnesses and corners, points and edges, by which we arrive at line again. From sight and touch, as we move about and pick up objects, we derive our knowledge of

27

space, volume, solid, mass weight, texture, hardness, softness, ascending, descending, diagonal, vertical, and so derive the geometry which is our mathematical model of physical reality.

It is not possible to separate drawing from painting, and we should not think of drawing as a preparation for painting. The technical limitations of certain mediums make it necessary to draw first and colour afterwards, but this is an artificial separation. Painting and drawing are one. Both start with the marks which we make on paper (or any other ground) with charcoal or brush or anything which makes a mark. If we are concerned with the kind of marks which we make rather than their colour, then we can discuss them as drawing. The drawn line shows quite simply that painting is a language of signs.

Line

Line does not have a physical existence. It is an idea initially mathematical, corresponding to the direction of a movement, the distance between two points or the boundary of an area. In art, line is used symbolically to express movement and to define objects (and their relationships) in the same way that in Euclidean geometry it is used to define figures. But where a formal geometry extracts only mathematical relationships, art retains the sensation at the source of experience, and where mathematics generalizes, art also describes particular events. The eye moves along the line of a hill or seizes the contour of a man or a tree, the hand explores the edge of a plank or grasps the shape of a cube. But the line is not a part of the hill or the plank. The line is the gesture which the hand makes in following the eye along the silhouette of the hill, in surrounding the shape of the man with a contour, in feeling the edges of the plank, or the changes of plane in the cube, in recalling the movement of the wave or the shape of an animal. *The drawn line is the record of the movement of the hand describing objects and their behaviour.*

From a tactile point of view the point is where the finger tip touches, the line is the finger moving over the object (describing a section); the flat hand covers and describes the plane; the fingers feel the line which is the edge of the plane. From a visual point of view the finger describes the contour shape, the eye (or rather the mind through the eye) behaves like a finger in following the contour. The eye follows and the finger describes the flight of the bird. The finger mimes the animal or the bird. It is a profound yet simple step to mime the animal or the bird with a mark on the wall or a finger moving in the dust. It is a further profound step to discover interior lines which suggest over-

'Bull's Head'. Wall painting at Lascaux

lapping shapes and marks which will symbolize the sections and changes of plane within an object. At each successive stage towards the skill we know as drawing, tactile and visual experience have been inseparable and at each step the natural mimetic gesture and the logic of geometry combine.

The line as gesture

The gestures of life are selected, simplified and translated into line in order to describe the significance of events according to their structure, character and movement. The gestures of the theatre in dance and mime use the same imaginary line by which patterns of movement are understood. *But the line which translates the event also transmits the emotion.* The gestures of an angry man are not the same as the gestures of a frightened man, or a man mourning or a man in love. The line which interprets the event in structure (geometry) and in character (mime) is also the arabesque to which the heart responds. It speaks of the emotion appropriate to the event and also reveals what the artist feels and something of his personality.

The line may be more explicit or less explicit. But the way in which the painter puts his marks on the paper is the full revelation of how he thinks and feels – the frankest revelation because it is the most intimate, inseparable from his own personality. Colour and shape he can deliberately choose, but the marks which he makes to put them down are a part of himself and can never be fully conscious. *The first measure of quality in a painting is the quality of line.* It is here that dishonesty, vanity, cowardice, laziness or courage and intelligence will show. There is no better start to a criticism of one's own work and no better way to start to read a master than response to line. It is equally true that colour conveys emotion, but colour conveys emotion as a general state of mind. It is line which conveys with peculiar force a specific emotion, and emotions which can be attached to objects or characteristics or events; because it is from gesture not colour that in ordinary life we can read other people's emotions, moods and characters, and we carry this animal gift with us into the field of art. In drawing, then, the line is in the mind. It is not in nature but read into nature. But also it must be realized the line is *not on the paper*. For ordinary purposes we talk about a drawn line where a line is intended, but there are only *marks* on the paper: the drawn line is *seen as a line because the mark is seen as conveying a gesture*. If it did not convey anything we would not see it as a line. We call it a line because it is a mark which records a movement. Of course a thin mark suggests a line but a thick mark or a fat brush

Carpet pattern, Asia Minor, sixteenth century

Victoria and Albert Museum, London

29

Hokusai: Mangwa Book IV.
Descriptive line leads us by
suggestion beyond what is
actually depicted

stroke equally contains a line in the movement of the direction of the
brush stroke; and the ragged edge of an area of paint or broken
touches equally contain line. Where the eye connects points along the
axis of a shape or a movement, line is also implied. In painting, the
brush mark takes on the graphic and expressive role of the line. but
directly we use a brush we see the line as running through and across
the shape and not simply round the edge of it.

The drawn line is an invention which is as impressive as the wheel or
the steam engine. By drawing, man has extended his ability to see and
comprehend what he sees in the same way that by extending his
vocabulary he has been able to enlarge his concepts. Without the
words the thoughts cannot come. Words are tools which enable us to
play with thought. In the same way, by drawing man has extended
his power of visual imagery, and his ability to sort and find meaning
in what he sees. But words and images are also not separable. (In

passing let us note that painting and literature are not antipathetic but complementary – if they were not we would have no writing yet. Intellectual activity is equally plastic and verbal. The symbolic languages are interchangeable, and at an unconscious level the images are one.)

Calligraphy

In China and Japan drawing and writing are much more closely related than in Europe. Writing is the mother of the arts. '.... The script represents the unbroken diagram of a dance. It is the dance of the hand, of the arms, of the fingers .... This dance does not speak only to our intuition through its qualities of elegance, power and sensibility; it also speaks a precise language of the intellect.

'Thus calligraphy, which with us is the science of dunces, in the Far East is the mother of the arts. A single tool – the brush – unites painting and writing.'*

Japanese ideograph for colour

The Chinese character is an ideograph which is modified from a more pictorial origin or composed from signs to which meaning has already been attached. The result is a system of marks which in addition to their use as logical symbols penetrate 'the heart through the eyes'. In Western poetry the basic meaning of words is enlarged by the music of their sound. But in China and Japan it is also the appearance of the words which exalts the sense with its hidden abstract meaning. If we appreciate the visual importance of calligraphy to the East it will be easier to see how all painting carries an abstract message in addition to or even in spite of what it represents. It is not surprising that Chinese characters have influenced abstract painting, since they are the most developed abstract art form which carries a precise as well as a poetic meaning. The brush marks accurately fill the space, complying with traditional proportions, but with a flow and freedom which admit the personality and comment of the calligrapher. There is a logical meaning, and an object to be contemplated. The design is flat on the paper, illustrating in its purest form those qualities of surface design which drawings and paintings in depth must also retain. Once a black mark is made on a white sheet of paper, the whole sheet is animated; white spaces mean as much as the black marks. Drawing is always design. Whatever sort of line or mark we make on paper it animates and alters the white page. The symbol, the meaning and the expression are equally in the black and in the white, in the brush mark and the space between, in the objects drawn and the spaces between the objects.

Yoshige Saito: 'Pittura 2'.
Relief painting by a contemporary Japanese artist

* *The sign in Japanese writing*, Fosco Moraini, Ark 22

31

A Catalan Nativity, twelfth
century. A simple repetitive sign
language is made eloquent by
cunning placing against a
quartered background and
by the sophisticated pattern
of varying curves which
a thick outline allows

Archaeological Museum, Diocese of Solsona

The line as a symbol by analogy

In our own art, we must not underrate the common origin of drawing
and writing. Apes and infants scraping in the dust make straight lines,
curves, wavy lines and the circular line that closes on itself. With awe
primitive man and children name these as the spear and the bow, the
serpent or water, the net or the cross roads, the moon or man, grasping
at reality with these first symbols in the magical twilight of their
endeavour to control themselves and their environment. The mark is
made first and endowed with meaning. Each symbol stands for many
things. We can see how the shapes and lines in a naturalistic painting
draw on an immemorial inheritance of unconscious meaning and poetic
evocation; and from where the cryptic sign language of abstract art

draws its power. Whether in the forgotten garden of scorpions on a Persian carpet, or in a painting by Paul Klee, the hook, the grid, the stick, signs for human artifacts and natural events recur: circles. rectangles and crosses – the emblems of flowers, stars, clouds and beasts.

Not only the abstract painting, which is deliberately painted as an ideogram on the surface of the canvas, but all paintings contain in the detail of surface pattern or the arrangement of the whole composition shapes of archetypal significance.

Line as a logical symbol: contour

To put a line round something is to name it and to attempt to enumerate its characteristics. It is a form of definition. Children arrive at the same time at a stage when they draw objects and when they name them.

33

It is difficult for any of us to draw in line something which we cannot name – that is to put a line round something which we cannot separate intellectually from its surroundings. If we draw a nameless thing, we automatically ask what it is while we draw it, and attempt to see a likeness in it to something which we can name. Both to draw things and to name things are attempts to identify and understand objects, situations, conditions and relationships. A particular function of line in drawing is (like naming) to define objects. With a line we first draw nouns. Later we describe relationships: physical situations, the geometry of space, psychological situations, movement. In the traditional European school of drawing (the heritage from Masaccio, through Raphael to Ingres), contour defines objects and gives them their precise structure and character, while tone (shading) is largely used to state generalities of form – the physical characteristics which all objects share alike – planes and structural relationships, space, lighting conditions. A cube or a cylinder may be given solidity by tone, but it is defined as a cube or a cylinder by line. Whenever we wish to give individuality, precise definition and character to a figure in life drawing or to a head or anything else which we put in a drawing, we find that we must pursue the contour ruthlessly and search out the form by means of outline. The more particular we wish to be the more ruthless we must be. The characteristic shape is in the contour. If in a painting we see a line which is enclosed we presuppose an object and try to recognize what it is.

Modelling and the tradition of objective drawing

The traditional combination of line with tonal modelling developed as a means of examining the physical world objectively. It is associated with optical systems of perspective and anatomical research. From the modern point of view this method of drawing remains the intellectual exercise by which we train ourselves to observe and think plastically in terms of the dimensions of space (and time). It provides an objective and scientific way of exploring and developing our own sensitivity to physical relationships. Most modern painters demonstrate a belief that painting is concerned with volumes and relationships in space. Although we may eventually choose colour or calligraphy as our means of expression, it is important first of all to command the use of tone (light and shade) to model 'form' (solid shape). This was never a question of modelling certain forms in order to make them 'look solid', but of relating volumes accurately in space: the three-dimensional space left between objects becomes as important as the objects them-

selves. The degree to which each form is modelled (and therefore
given its sculptural projection) must correspond to the space which
contains it. By modelling the solids so that their parts are related and
so that each solid is related, the three-dimensional space between is
also considered and modelled. If we look at a seated figure which is
facing us, it is the space in the angle between the torso and the pro-
jecting thighs which must be 'carved' out; the space under the chair in
the angle between the lower leg and the flat plane of the floor. This
is a sculptural conception, and the means used are borrowed from
sculpture. If a cast (or monochrome statue) is lit from one side or above
the lighting reveals the shape. If we look only for those changes of
tone which indicate shape, ignoring any accidents of light (shine, for
instance, or the darker texture of a pitted surface) and changes of

colour, we can then use corresponding tonal changes in our drawing of the cast to symbolize only the shapes we see. I say *symbolize* because if we are to give maximum effect to the volumes which the changes of tone on the cast enable us to see, we will not do so by attempting to copy the tones we see exactly, but by placing the changes we see in their *order of importance* as indications of volume. We cannot put down all the changes we see but only those which are most significant of shape.

1. From our own experience and from the study of drawings which have followed this method, we will find that slight indications of change where we see the shape 'turn', suggest volume far more easily than a heavy tonal rendering.

2. The changes in the light side are as important as the changes in the dark side. A form is turning all the time.

3. Against a stronger dark the white paper seems lighter. By using this law of 'simultaneous contrast' we can bring a point in the drawing nearer to us or by reducing contrast we can take it further away.

4. By indicating the point on any rounded form which is nearest to us and the changes of plane receding from it, we describe the section through as well as the surface.

There are many other factors which are only revealed in the progressive development of a series of drawings. These points have been picked out to show that by using line for contour, and tone to model the interior (and of course tying the two together), we have developed a system of *logical symbols* for controlling volume and representing objects related in space. Visual experience is both selected and transposed purposely. The ability to model lightly is stressed because it is most important to painting. Almost all students who have learnt to draw before they start to paint model in tones which are too contrasted, so that in composing they lose control of the areas of light and dark. Another common fault is to balloon certain objects at the expense of spatial relationship. Obviously if the three-dimensional aspect of one object is overstated it can throw out the balance of volumes in the whole painting. These are cases where the acquisition of a formal skill gets out of hand. Painting and drawing should surely not be separated but studied together, so that the painter can arrive at the skill he needs as he requires it and not in an academic vacuum in advance of his natural development.

The expression 'logical symbol' is used deliberately because the relationship between the objects drawn and line and tone which repre-

Rubens: 'A Woman Churning'

Devonshire Collection, Chatsworth

sent them is as precisely logical as that between words and their meaning. Neither spoken nor written words are any longer like the objects and situations which they represent and it is therefore obvious to us that the connection between them, because it is not imitative and naturalistic, must be symbolic and, insofar as words always mean the same thing, logical. The interesting thing about traditional European drawing is that the most naturalistic drawing is also the least directly imitative. In case anyone is confused by this it is recalled that neither line nor tone exist in nature (visual experience). The one is a descriptive gesture, the other comes from sculpture (tactile experience); if some of us see like this it is because we read nature like this. It is a method of analysing and manipulating visual data which is acquired. It is very difficult to persuade the ordinary man that drawing in this objective and formal sense is not a natural gift which his fairy godmother forgot, but something which has to be learnt the hard way and that it takes at least two years to break the ice. It is equally difficult to persuade him that drawings and paintings have to be read. A difficult book he shuts after the first page and leaves to better men, but a painting he can see at one glance and fondly imagines that he knows what it is about and why he does or does not like it.

But just as words are not simply logical symbols but part of a living and developing language with all sorts of overtones and cross currents of meaning, so the most conceptual of the Masters' drawings are often also the most human and intuitive. The conceptual element is only one element in any drawing, and the drawing which is most aware of intellectual structure can also be a drawing of the immediate sensation of life, and deeply moving. The formal machinery of great European draughtsmen – line, modelling, planes, foreshortening, perspective, anatomy of structure, function and movement, taking their place with colour in scientific systems of composition – is more than a grammar of logical symbols to aid representation. That is an accidental by-product. As the consequence of a profound and continuous enquiry into the nature of reality, in which many of the greatest minds of all times took part, the methods which they used were in themselves a developing system of logic; and one which remains valid in exactly the same way that past philosophers or scientists (whose hypotheses no longer precisely apply to events and whose ideas have long been absorbed into our moral climate) still profoundly affect the currents of our beliefs and actions. The adulation given to Michelangelo by his contemporaries was not for a 'great artist' in the modern sense (that art is separate from real issues and genius is to be stored in museums and gaped at by tourists). They believed that they had among themselves one of the greatest intellects who had ever lived, whose communications mattered. Between the time of Giotto and that of Rembrandt there are a good many we might rate as high. It is this which makes it possible to experience from the finest drawings the same excitement which is stimulated by the disciplined formulation of concepts when reading Descartes or Kant or the satisfaction of a scientific theory neatly demonstrated. We study these masters in exactly the same way that a philosopher or a physicist or an economist must study the essential history of his subject.

But it was not only among primitive peoples that gestures or geometric patterns evoked deeper unconscious responses – by correspondence to the hidden imagery of symbol, analogy and association. The mathematical systems of perspective and composition of Renaissance painting which expound structure objectively in depth were also the formulae which would unlock the secrets of universal harmony and discord, and guide the human soul beyond into hidden places. These were also times when line, shape and colour came as words did to Marlowe and Shakespeare at the spring-tide of the English language, taking on rhetorical magnificence, swollen with a burden of symbolic meaning, and flooded with personal associations and conceits newly invented or re-created from ancient sources. Christian and pagan tradition alike (the holy fathers and mystics, neo-Platonism, sacred legend, classical mythology, Byzantine doctrine, echoes of mystery religion and residues of Eastern heresy, even the cult of the *trouvères*) confirmed that there is an esoteric as well as an exoteric understanding of every image – all signs have an inner as well as an overt meaning: there are layers of understanding. Tradition openly asserts that images include intuitive knowledge which the intellect cannot penetrate; if we owe to the men of the Renaissance an incredible richness of formal vocabulary because they were prepared to penetrate as far as the the intellect would go, it was not at the expense of intuitive and unconscious meaning.

Parallel to the formal exploration of physical reality came that other side to Italian art, mystical, mythological and legendary, above all allegorical. We underrate its importance because it extends to modes of thought which are now virtually lost to us. We appreciate the intensity of emotion which ripples the smooth varnished surfaces but not the obsessions which roused this intensity – the terrors, cravings and

Braque: 'The Purple Tablecloth'

joys which rise as shadowy monsters from the pool below. We appreciate 'surface tension' or 'significant form' or whatever the art books have told us. Flowing line, pellucid colour, logical design, all the serene formal values which move us gently now and to which we attribute the qualities we admire, are surface echoes of bitter psychic conflicts long forgotten.

Planes

One further convention must be fully understood. The plane is a structural concept derived from Euclidean geometry. Originally the side of a solid figure, it also does not exist in but is read into nature. Its meaning has been greatly extended by painters. First of all, in conceptual drawing, planes are a way of reading the human figure or landscape as if they were solid geometry. In this sense planes establish tactile rather than visual relationships, and the surface of any object can be seen as an infinite succession of changing planes. Relationships in space can be seen as planes receding behind each other or planes set parallel and at angles to each other. In formal perspective the visual field is ruled by planes – the ground plane, the picture plane, the vertical, horizontal and diagonal planes of objects – in an attempt to unify tactile and optical experience by Euclidean symbols. From here planes become large areas of colour or small brush strokes which describe a relationship in space by reference to each other and to the surface of the canvas – the '*plans colorés*' of the Post-Impressionists. The importance of the plane still lies in the fact that it is the symbol for expressing a tactile sensation in a visual form. It is significant that in contemporary paintings, although formal perspective and Euclidean space have now been abandoned, planes remain firmly entrenched as the means of manipulating formal relationships within a painting without necessarily any correspondence to physical experience. They are part of the historic language of Western painters and it is impossible to work in a literate idiom without fully understanding their use.

Intuition

It is not the convention which matters, but how it is used. If we make a descriptive line drawing of a simple branch, it will be inadequate unless it indicates the way the branch has grown and how that branch comes to be supported and suspended in the air. In the end a kind of knowledge is required that goes beyond scientific observations, which will always come to us in separate parcels, while we have to sum up the actuality of the moment. Structure cannot simply be a static Euclidean analysis. Anatomy must include the elements of growth and of movement in time, the energy which makes the tree grow. A drawing can never be about one moment only but must be about a complex of experience. We cannot know how the tree grew except by relating what we see to our own innate sense of growth, or how the branch hangs in the air without identifying it with our own innate sense of balance and our own weight, or how the wind rocks it without ourselves feeling the wind blow. Intuitively even the most ordinary child will draw the most wonderful and convincing things! Somehow we must become the branch before we can draw the branch – to represent, whether direct from nature or from memory, demands identification and a return to the intuitive and spontaneous gesture of primitive mime; and to draw well we must write down the immediate truth as it comes to us without regard for structural formulae and academic scruples about the method we use.

This problem of representation remains the problem of every painter, since every painting must mean something (an abstract painting must have an abstract meaning; it must represent an idea or a sensation). At its simplest the problem is this: we can paint a rough orange circle and it precisely evokes an orange; we can then add solidity, light and shade, porous texture, cast shadow, colour in shadow – adding one observed detail after another until it looks like nothing on earth. Obviously likeness depends not on copying detail but on striking some chord of recognition within ourselves by economical means; whatever we are trying to paint – an idea, a fact, sensations or physical situations, objects in light or relationships of pure colour – demands a synthesis which corresponds to this inner image, in the medium of paint. In the end we find we cannot paint an orange, but some qualities of an orange, a comment on an orange, something which an orange stands for. The painter comes to read external experience intuitively in terms of an image and in terms of his medium. (But it is the painter's inability to cope with the object as such that has brought us to the point of murdering it.)

Distortion

Whatever contour we see, the line we draw is selected from it imaginatively. The same contour is subject to an infinite number of variations. No two people, or ourselves, can draw it twice the same. If we look at the contour of a leaf, part of the human body, or a hill, we can see immediately how indeterminate nature is. By noting straight and curve, sharp curve and soft curve, large curve and small, we must carve a way along that line, simplifying the chaos which will overwhelm us if we lose ourselves in detail. We cannot put in every movement of the line and so we must choose the movement which has meaning. It is literally madness to leave the choice to luck. Whether it is line or shape or colour, we must decide on relationships, and from the sort of decisions which we make the character of a painting proceeds – on from the first coloured marks. Knowledge provides us with alternatives, but the choice must be intuitive as well as rational. To distort is to ignore an inexpressive, irrational and commonplace norm, which corresponds to no fact and no act of imagination.

Scale

The relative sizes which the eyes see are not those which the brain accepts. If we draw on a sheet of glass the outline of the objects which we see through it, we produce proportions which are true to the eye considered mechanically as a lens. But if we look at our visual field in a normal way, the eye moving over it continually, examining, recognizing and relating, we adjust what we see towards what we know to be there (or what we imagine or wish to be there). We form an image in which relative sizes may be quite different.

A good example is a landscape with distant mountains. A photograph will show the mountains as a shallow line of humps behind the large shapes of the middle distance and the even larger masses of the foreground. But what our eye perceives are mountains towering above the landscape. We leap the foreground, denigrate the middle distance, and the mind's eye – the mental image which we form – enlarges the mountain and rearranges the landscape to agree with our factual reading of what it contains. In addition the mountains may have an emotional impact, or the trees and flowers in the foreground may appeal to us; we will see larger what interests us most. When we paint this landscape, both consciously and unconsciously we will interpret the scale to give it meaning and mood. If we enlarge the mountains then their lines will relate quite differently to the foreground; also we will have to fit in more foreground and less mountains. We may have started by following our instincts but we are soon engaged in composing a picture.

Changes of scale are perhaps the most important and (in academic training) the most neglected means of expression. Freedom to compose is offered us by the alternative ways of seeing – according to sight, according to knowledge or according to feeling. If we look across the room at the meeting of floor and wall, we can see either vertical or horizontal larger or smaller according to where we focus our attention. If we look at objects or the interval between them, their relative sizes change. In ordinary circumstances interest guides our sense of scale. In painting this interest must be purposive. The figure composition of the Old Masters illustrates the freedom with which they exercised their right to ring these changes.

Drawing in paint

The elegant and expressive but continuous line of the Italian and Flemish primitives which surrounds and defines objects while giving movement to the design was a consequence of technical limitations. Tempera, glue size or oil above tempera necessitated layers of relatively transparent colour on top of a set drawing; true frescoes, although painted spontaneously into wet plaster so that colour and drawing were one, demanded an accurate full-scale preparatory cartoon. Drawing came before colour. The precise conceptual use of line and

Rembrandt: detail

National Gallery, London

tone belongs to the time when painting and drawing were separated. Oil paint offered painters a flexible medium in which drawing and colour are united in the same brush stroke. Successive painters have developed their own shorthand, drawing with a point or chalk or brush, in which outline and interior forms are modelled by economical marks of any sort. Rembrandt, Goya, Delacroix or Degas show how the calligraphic mark and broken contour replace continuous lines and gradations of tone; their drawing relates to paintings in which the brush mark inside the shape is as expressive as the linear contour. The painter who is to use oil paint fully must be able to draw across and through separate shapes, and to paint the background into the object and the object into the background freely. The danger of learning to draw with a continuous contour is that we end by painting up to the edge of each shape and produce paintings of separate unrelated objects. The broken contour allows a passage through from one shape to the next and the choice between interior lines (the edges of areas of tone and of planes) and outer contour. The freedom offered by alternative solutions cannot be refused. This plastic and graphic freedom which we accept as painterly developed through Titian, El Greco, Velasquez, Rembrandt and Rubens.

Nowadays we do not find Rubens altogether to our taste. He is at once too skilled and too fleshy. *But he is our Technical Master*. It is worth coming to an understanding with him, even if it means cultivating our historical sense to get inside his athletic skin. He is a better man than ourselves, more thorough in his sensuality, more ruthless in the use of his intellect, alarming because he suggests that the men of his age were stauncher than ourselves and without self-pity. Technically he made it possible to draw and colour in one act. El Greco, Velasquez and Rembrandt contributed as much to this revolution, but Rubens, meeting the demands of his age (as Baroque decorator) and those of his own personal homespun vision, finding in this antithesis the extension of his own intellect and ranging imagination, produced a method of painting which has been a source of information to all painters since. Even the painters who go back to the primitives for design or imagery cannot forget his fluent calligraphy. Few still draw and fill in. But Rubens' thin darks and loaded lights have allowed us to build up a painting (thick and thin, at one coup or over a number of sittings) with fluidity, flexibility and generosity of paint, to paint slow or fast and to write the picture in at the speed which corresponds to the development of our thoughts, so that the form, colour, movement and quality of paint are one. Historically the idea of painterliness owes most to Rubens.

The richness of European painting (and to me its superiority over Eastern art) lies in the full-bodied rendering of physical sensation. The development of the technical possibilities of oil paint and the Western urge to master the material world have combined to produce a form of art in which the painting itself has a powerful physical presence, appealing to the intelligence through the senses.

In many kinds of modern painting, strong brush strokes (or knife marks), whether assisting or contradicting the representational theme, complementing or countering line and form, have an expressive

De Kooning: 'Woman I', 1950-1952

Museum of Modern Art, New York

quality of their own. Of contemporary painters, De Kooning particularly illustrates the way in which the charged surface becomes a continuous stretch of interlocking texture and colour. The historical debt is owed to Rubens for speed of execution and continuity of surface, and to Rembrandt for the alliance of impasto and intensity of vision. The way leads back through Picasso's physical attack and inventive imagery, and Van Gogh's direct handwriting.

The background to contemporary painting

The Old Masters provide objective starting points from which later painters discover their own handwriting and against which they can test their own sensations. Cézanne substituted colour for tone, Van Gogh calligraphic marks for interior modelling. Their inventions with those of Monet, Seurat and Gauguin have led to almost all the developments of contemporary painting. They reinterpreted the conceptual images of the Old Masters in the terms of the direct sensation of the Impressionists. Summing up both the tradition and the revolution, they became the watershed from which the increasingly specialized rivulets of modern painting flow, and in them we first glimpse primitive and oriental sources which have produced the spate of new influences, from past ages and distant lands as the world grows smaller and the tombs open – Malraux's 'Museum without Walls'.

Van Gogh in this instance is an extremely interesting example of how a painter finds among conflicting influences the means to suit his purpose. Passionately devoted to the reality of what he saw and at the same time with an inner compulsion (egged on by Gauguin's symbolist theory) to achieve symbolic meaning in pure colour; true to Rembrandt and too literal to banish the tonal differences which he saw; devoted to the strong light which exalted him and faithful to Impressionist doctrine, therefore unable to falsify the lighting condition (against the light, with the light, three-quarter lit, half lit, however it happened to be); he was compelled to find some way of reducing the dark tonal areas which he had used in his earlier paintings before he discovered colour and which would break the fullness and spread of his colour, destroying its impact. Aware that he could not have both colour and tone to the full he used the calligraphic mark (in complementary colour) and the thick brush stroke as a substitute for modelling. He literally wrote the form down.

The ikon painter could ignore tone and lighting condition; Vermeer controlled the lighting to suit his composed balance of light, dark and local colour. Van Gogh holds in suspension the dilemma of the

Van Gogh: 'The House of
Vincent at Arles'

Collection of V. W. van Gogh, Laren

modern because he has both accepted the reality of the appearance and
also found an abstract equivalent in pure colour, as if it were music.
Present painters, unable to compose in the face of nature, feel compelled either to pursue complete abstraction or to accept appearances
literally: Van Gogh faced nature and did both. The problem is this:
if we reject modelled form, we reject chiaroscuro, chief weapon in the
armoury of the Old Masters in composing. The primitive, using a
continuous line and local colour, has no way of softening the passage
through from the shape of one object to another, and therefore he
cannot join two objects together easily to form a new shape. He
cannot separate one part of an object by shadow from another, joining
if he wishes the dark or light side to other dark or light shapes. He

47

cannot weave the weft of light and dark due to the lighting condition through the warp of light and dark local tones. Each coloured and drawn area coincides and must remain intact. It is difficult for him to vary the scale of his compositional unit; it must remain the scale of coloured shapes and therefore of the objects to which these precisely correspond. Even more serious, with unbroken contour he cannot make continuous space. These are the problems of the closed line, which contains an object and separates it from its surroundings. Freedom to compose forms musically and elastically in space demands the broken shape and the waves of shadow that can subtly eat away the contour. In rejecting as mechanical and academic the older recipes which involved a compromise between tone and colour, and shape and line (but made use of them all), in favour of a direct and combined statement of shape and colour, we tie ourselves rigidly to objects – the last thing which any modern conscious of the relativity of existence would wish to do. Alternatively we may be condemned never to make a precise and explicit statement – always to use the vague shape. Like Van Gogh's landscapes, Monet's 'Water Lilies' (National Gallery) shows a way out of this difficulty. The tonal scale is so abbreviated that we are only dealing with colour against colour, and since these painters accepted the right offered to all of us by the Impressionists to see anything any colour we like – by playing local colour (and its complementary) against the colour of light (and its complementary) – the passage through from one object to another is achieved by colour. Contours can be found and lost in terms of colour and broken brush strokes. But there is a danger of monotony from lack of tonal variety; no sonorous darks, no brilliant lights, no subtle half tones and half colours – none of the beautiful greys, which become colour by juxtaposition and are the stock in trade of the tonal painter, offering repose between excitation. Brilliant colour without tonal difference may excite but tire. Monet however sustained his colour by an intensity of emotion which accompanies a vision that is strictly impartial. He is not descending to the vulgarity of colour for colour's sake! He is writing down an interpretation of a visual experience. Monet commands the respect of a modern not just because he presupposes abstract Impressionism by forty-five years: nothing seems more improbable than that the nineteenth-century prettiness of the lily pool should become the blueprint for a ruthless and elemental modernism. These are not the haphazard variegations of *tachiste fondant*, nor is Monet concerned with romantic sentiments. Old and moving to blindness he finds in this dragonfly

Monet: 'Water Lilies', detail

world the perfect example of the relativity of physical substance as an analogue of the brevity of man's existence. This dissolving world is only held together by the effort of the painter's will expressed through the analytical severity of his eye. The physical landscape has become an interior landscape, but strictly mapped out as if by a draughtsman-naturalist on a geographical expedition.

Scientific theory of colour

Modern versions of colour theory date from Chevreuil and the Impressionists. From that time quite useful approximations to fact – the colour circle, primary and secondary colours, warm and cold colours and especially complementary colours – rapidly became a commonplace of student training.

But there is a gap in scientific colour theory which needs to be filled. How does the eye sort and see colour? Assuming that it registers certain primary colours first and derives the rest from them, what are these primary colours? What are normally called primary colours are a matter of empirical convenience, according to the practical end in view: a printer using photographic filters produces his range of colour from red, blue and green. With opaque pigment, we must use red, blue, yellow. Transparencies for coloured lights require a different red, blue and green, while a physicist using the spectrum to identify elementary substances in a source of light may think in terms of seven primary distinctions.

For practical convenience the painter finds available certain alternative pigments which closely approach six obvious changes in the spectrum. From these he chooses those which are convenient and to his taste to treat as primary colours. He takes into consideration permanence as well as convenience in mixing. Equally or more valuable are certain earth pigments such as light red, Indian red, yellow ochre, siennas and umbers which are of great permanence as well as beauty. Although according to colour theory these might be considered secondary colours they have intensity as well as subtlety, and a degree of saturation which cannot be achieved by mixing a near primary pigment with black, or two near primaries together. Each painter chooses his palette from available fast pigments and that is his keyboard. Whatever theoretical value he gives to tables of primary, secondary and tertiary mixtures, or mixtures of tones produced by a colour with black or white, in practice he will use and memorize the effect of some eight or twelve actual pigments, and their permutations, and will visualize a colour scheme in terms of these actual pigments and their behaviour. Schematic ranges of colours corresponding to perceptible differences of wavelength are of value in industry where accurate mechanical matching is required, but of little practical use to most artists. Differences of tone measured by quantities of added black or white are visually unreliable because the bias of the black or white towards blue or brown substantially alters hue as well as tone. Indian red with white alters towards violet and returns to pink as more white is added, vermilion with black changes towards violet or brown according to the black used. Addition of alizarin or burnt sienna is needed to keep a red red as darker tones are required. A sensitive eye cannot accept the simple addition of black.

I believe that most painters carry in their minds a number of colours of precise hue and tone which they like – perhaps a certain blue, a certain green, a brown and so on which approximate to the behaviour of mixtures of pigment which they habitually use and to the colour which they seek or find in visual experience. These are the colours which have meaning for them and which they build up into colour schemes which have meaning – corresponding to emotional and symbolic requirements. The work of most painters seems to suggest that for each period they use quite a limited number of colours and tones. Since a colour exists only in relation to other colours and each is continually modified by its neighbour, only a very limited range of chosen tones (of each hue) can properly be controlled. The equivalent of colour in nature can only be found by transposition.

Transposition

All good colour involves transposition. Transposition corresponds to selection and distortion in drawing. Transposition means alterations of tone – lighter or darker; of hue – warmer and colder; and the selection of the dominant and subsidiary colours in a colour scheme. A decisive choice must be made among vague alternatives. In working from nature it is particularly important to choose the colour of neutral half tones, since these must take on the colour which we read into them.

Whether we believe that we work with colour which we literally see or with colour which we seek to see, or with colour which we invent, these are all equally the result of our total past experience of colour and the combination of objective and subjective meanings which we give to colour. We can only recognize colour which has some meaning. By transposition we unite in one vision the colour which we believe we actually see and the colour which is required to give the whole painting meaning. Corot declared that he sought only tones – changes of hue were an added gift; Gauguin revived the symbolic language of pure colour. But whichever sort of selection we choose, it must partly take its meaning from similar colour schemes which have been used before. We derive colour from pigments, from observation and from art.

Local colour and lighting

As I write winter sun floods into my studio. The floor (in accordance with the lease) is carpeted with a felt which is now a dirty yellow. One wall has a paper of Chinese vermilion, and a patch of sunlight falling on this gives to the centre of the blue-grey shadow under my table an extraordinarily rich orange glow. In my field of vision this is the colour which excites my interest; it is the result of a reflection within a cast shadow. It is not a colour which I could easily imagine – unlike the man-made vermilion of the wallpaper, the black of the table or the dirty yellow of the floor. But the colour of carpet, wallpaper and the orange glow in the blue-grey of the shadow under the table are related to each other and to the intensity of the light with an absolute mathematical accuracy. As the sun goes in for a moment these colours change and their relationship changes. This is an illustration of the difference between local colour and colour conditioned by light. I easily recognize and can even name the colour of the wallpaper; the manufacturer intended it to be a certain red. The fact that it is quite a different colour where a patch of sunlight falls does not prevent me from reading his intention. We think of local colour as a property of objects which we can name. But a judgment about local colour is usually a judgment about pigmentation; it is always easier to be certain of the local colour of something which we can touch or handle. We have to view a distant mountain in several different lights before we can be certain of its colour. The change of colour where the patch of sunlight falls on the wall is an effect of light, while the glowing orange reflected from it in the shadow under the table is entirely a condition of a particular light. To note such differences is one of the strongest visual pleasures. The changes rung by light on even one single colour, and the power of shadow to contain colour, which is often more intense than the colours of objects themselves, but un-attached to objects and therefore curiously abstract, provide a natural experience not unlike music. We rejoice in light.

In order to define what we mean by local colour we might start by remarking that it is colour which belongs to an object or substance, and which we therefore consider to be one of its characteristics. But although objects of the same kind tend to similarity of colour and we recognize objects by their colour, it does not mean that a local colour is the colour which belongs to a class of objects. On the contrary the local colour of an object is the colour which belongs to that particular object – which may be like or very unlike the rest of its kind in colour (an extraordinarily green apple or a unique russet apple with a peculiar tinge of violet) and also a colour which belongs to that object at a particular moment in time and not necessarily at any other (the green apple may be gently rotting and be brown by tomorrow). Local colour is the contribution of the object itself to the total colour effect. We do not see local colour by itself, but it is one kind of relationship which we can look for in the colours which we see. We distinguish this aspect of colour from that aspect of colour which characterizes the lighting condition and the way that light is reflected from the various surfaces of an object or the atmosphere between ourselves and the object; we talk of a local colour as belonging to the object, but modified by the colour of the atmosphere or the lighting condition. We do not really see local colour at all; we think it and we read it. It is part of our technique for separating objects and identifying them, a means of classifying and understanding what we see. We have learnt to do this automatically – as if the eye did it and not the mind.

When we distinguish local colour, we are making a judgment about pigmentation or microscopic physical structure.

So strong is the habit of concentrating on local colour that the man who wishes to give detached attention to all the aspects of visual experience must train himself to counter it. Every painter knows how difficult it is to teach the layman to see colour with detachment. It was their disregard for local colour and for popular superstitions about colour (that tree trunks are always brown or bananas yellow) which once made the Impressionists so difficult to understand. Their contribution is still the first step towards a modern education in colour.

The eye and mind together are capable of extraordinarily fine distinctions of colour and make continual decisions as to the cause of these differences, noting changes of plane, of shape and of texture, of the colour and direction of light or relationships of mass in space, so that quite unconsciously we build up a mental picture which is a model of the physical nature of the view in front of us, on which we may base quite conscious decisions such as the direction in which we wish to walk or where we should apply the weedkiller.

What is remarkable in this is the ability of the eye (and that part of the mind linked with it) to read the causes of what it sees, distinguishing in colour painted surfaces from dyed fabrics, weathering from intrinsic colouring, transparency from glitter, opacity from limpidity, solid from liquid, vegetable from animal; leaf from fur and fur from feather; sky from water; solid from liquid from vapour; shadow from substance. The activities of the eye are intellectual activities. The very variety and subtlety of visually descriptive words in any language testifies to this.

Margaret Meade remarks that the Eskimos name some seventeen different kinds of white for snow. We know that different races and cultures name and appear to see quite different ranges of colour. A colour judgment is always about something other than colour; it is about the uses or effects, dangers or advantages of the substance coloured. We only see a colour when we are making such a judgment. The Eskimo distinguishes these different whites because he ascribes a practical value to each; one warns him of danger to his life, another is advantageous in hunting, one is bad for walking, another heralds a change of season. Artists in dissociating a colour from its environmental condition appear to treat it as an abstract quality but it still carries over into painting, to be used inventively in new contexts, factual information, symbolic meaning and emotional associations, some of which are common to mankind, some local to a particular culture, some personal to individual experience, some primitive and others highly cultivated. The language of colour is not at all abstract but extremely concrete and universal; meanings appear most uncertain when we are ignorant of their cultural background, most precise when we have a common history and personal sympathy with the colourist. If I am asked whether everyone sees the same colour my answer is 'of course not'; objective colour judgments are recordings of observed information: a man who can extract more information from a landscape will see more differences of colour; we do not *see colour* but acquire information which we record as colour. Local colour informs us about chemical structure, tone about physical structure, a certain quality of hue and tone about texture or weather or light. Equally someone with rich emotional responses and strong visual imagination will see more colour, and give to colour greater meaning related to historic or personal associations. Colour, like line, is not something we see, but a way of seeing. We see colour according to our ability to read and understand and relate past to present experience. A colour sense increases with practice. In painting, colour is always interpretation. The origins of emotional and symbolic interpretation are factual and from experience. Symbolic colour like the the language of dreams presents an idea in the form of a concrete

Gauguin: 'Le Pouldu'. It was this or a similar landscape which Kandinsky looked at, without at first recognizing any figurative content and which led him towards abstract painting

example; the meaning is concealed from the intellect, but instantly grasped by intuition. Mix for example in the range of red ochres a colour which corresponds to 'rust'. Ponder the associations with earth, iron ore, rusted metal, the colour of animals, lichens, autumnal vegetation and so on; then the corresponding man-made objects – plough-shares, ships, cranes, ancient artifacts discovered in gravel beds, cowhide, harness; the abstract ideas for which these might stand – industry, maritime adventure and wealth, decay and poverty, the curbing of natural forces. The same colour may take on a friendly or menacing aspect according to context. Alter the colour slightly to correspond to 'chestnut' or 'dried blood', and try again. Some nuance may prove too painful to allow an easy flow of images; the meaning is intense but buried. Free association of this kind demonstrates that our power to give shades of meaning is as acute as our powers of observation. There is nothing esoteric or mystical in colour symbolism.

We have made the distinction between local colour and conditional colour in observed experience. What does this distinction mean in painting? In painting we use the chemical colour of the pigment to symbolize all the different kinds of information which we receive from colour in nature.

1. In painting therefore all colour is, first of all, local colour, because it is the actual colour of the pigment used. A painting is always (and must be seen to be) a pattern on a flat surface. When we recognize the colour scheme of a painting, we are looking at the colour in its role as surface pattern; and this is what is meant when we say that Gauguin or Braque and Picasso in synthetic cubism localize colour. They give to colour its maximum effectiveness as surface pattern, reacting against the Impressionists who made great use of colour as a means of conveying a condition of light.

2. Colour conditioned by light is therefore to be associated with the representational element in painting, and is especially attractive to painters who are profoundly interested in visual sensation (Velasquez or Constable). Paintings which produce a visual equivalent of tactile sensation can rely on local colour and modelling as a logical symbol for sculptural solids. Paintings in flat tones of local colour allow the strongest symbolic significance. But in all paintings some degree of respect for condition of light and atmosphere exists. The Italian primitives may state a solid in local colour but the convincing sensation of space is due to that consistent envelope of light which surrounds the figures.

This is just as true for abstract painting as figurative. Relative opacity or translucency, weight, brilliance or dullness, darkness and lightness, suggestions of object and ground, cool and warm, give to each colour an implication which the eye will instinctively read in relationship to the visual experience by which we know the phenomenal world, in which consideration of light and atmosphere must to some degree be included. We can see how some abstract painters use colour in a way which is more localized than others. At one extremity we have Mondrian, at the other abstract expressionism standing for return to conditional colour. The distinction between abstract (or non-figurative) and figurative painting lies in the attempt that abstract painters make to use formal relationship while eliminating the object. The object (the horse, the man, the tree) is created by representational means (whether

Velasquez: 'The Infanta Margareta Teresa'. Although intent on visual truth, Velasquez did not sacrifice the decisive pattern of local tone and colour which is the secret of traditional pictorial construction

Kunsthistorisches Museum, Vienna

basic symbols or naturalistic) and some abstract painters have equally attempted to eliminate all those other representational elements which signify the conditions in which objects exist. Of these light is the most potent. It is the mathematical precision with which all the hues and tones of colour in nature are related, which in a moment of insight into the laws governing visual experience gives us the detached sensation of physical beauty. Such moments of aesthetic enjoyment are an abstract assessment of nature parallel to the enjoyment of a work of art, detached to some degree from the ordinary meaning of objects and situations in our struggle for existence. The sensation of visual and tactile unity is derived from the continuity of space and solid presented by planes directed to and from the light and the changes of tone and colour which reveal these to us. In any attempt to produce pictorial unity it is difficult to imagine a satisfactory solution to a scheme of colour which does not produce an ordering of colour equivalent to that produced by the laws which govern the relationships produced by a lighting condition. Our apparently *a priori* knowledge of these laws and our ability to organize colour is based on our total visual and tactile experience; the symbolic and emotional associations which give to certain combinations of colour the most significance must have been acquired on the one hand from visual experience and on the other from our own play with colour and the symbolic meanings which have been given to colours within our own culture, that is to say, from art. It is easy to imagine how the vision of a child taken from an early age to services in a Byzantine cathedral can be affected by a quality of colour which is itself art. El Greco may have been such a child. But every child experiences this in his home, where nature and art are one and where art and utility are inseparable. By art man reshapes his environment, and art of one sort or another provides the larger part of our background. By colour especially we make immediate aesthetic changes in our surroundings, decorating, furnishing and gardening. With coloured carpets the nomad makes a garden in the desert. Perhaps our sense of colour has developed even more from experiment with pigments and dyes than from observation. The meaning and the emotional flavour given to colour derives from our environment and from the traditions and experiments of art. We start with a pigment and make it an equivalent to something we see. But a sense of the unifying relationships given to colour by light must feed to some degree into the secret mythology of colour hidden in the deep and inarticulate caverns of the mind. The initial choice of a colour scheme in a high or low key corresponds both to a lighting condition and to a state of mind.

Tone

By tone we mean the lightness or darkness of a colour (see *Basic Design* by Maurice de Sausmarez). In fact it is the quantity or intensity of light reflected from an object (as in a photograph) and we can separate this in our minds from the hue of a colour. We must distinguish between local tone (the self-tone of an object and an aspect of its local colour) and tone which is due to the way in which light is falling on an object. Visually this is affected by:

1. The direction of light and the shape of the object (surface planes). Turned to the source of light will be lighter planes, turned away will be darker ones. Planes on which reflected light falls will be modified and some degree lighter.

2. Texture. According to the direction of the light and the nature of the texture, tone is altered by texture. A heavy texture is generally darker than a smooth surface. Trees tend to be darker than grass, grass darker than plough.

3. The local colour (the darker or lighter tone of the object itself)

4. Distance and atmosphere

In extreme lighting conditions differences of local tone are lost. All darks tend to become equally dark.

In painting tone is used:

1. To model objects

2. As local tone (the lightness or darkness of a local colour)

3. To render the effect of lighting conditions

4. As chiaroscuro – composition by light and shade

Light and dark are always powerful elements in design; but chiaroscuro especially applies to paintings in which a flow of strong lights and darks countering naturalistic forms gives the painter an additional means of abstract organization; examples are Caravaggio, Ribera, Rembrandt, La Tour. But the extreme use of light and dark may be at the expense of colour and even form.

All painting involves a tonal scheme; there is a choice between the use of strong colour and strong distinctions of tone. We cannot use both equally at once. Many of the great masters – Breughel for example – use a discreet combination of both, balancing strength of colour against strength of tone and separating strong local colour with neutral warm and cold areas. Many moderns from Gauguin to Rothko illustrate the rule that colours are most effective when close in tone.

Values

In French *ton* (*tons*) means colour (colours); *valeurs* means tones. Painting by values therefore literally means painting by tones. In academies this theory became debased by the influence of photography to mean painting from nature in photographic tones: tone in this sense is separated from colour and, provided that the tone is visually correct, the colour does not matter, with the result that acceptable tones are arrived at by dilution of colour by black. This degenerate theory led to the copying of degrees of light and dark only. French ideas tend to develop as theoretical synthesis where English thought tends to the analysis of empirical experience; the French do not appear to have ever separated the idea of tone from the idea of colour, so that painting by values in France has meant painting by the just tone of particular colours. Colour and tone are one. The value includes the saturation (intensity) of the colour as well as its degree of brightness; the hue of the colour does not lose its importance. The value is a value of a colour, not a tone value separated from its colour. A colour has tone (lighter or darker), saturation (intensity) and hue (red or blue, warmer or colder.) The first two represent its value. The importance of the value of colours is not that it allows accurate copying of visual relationships but that colours can be related in space. We must look at Corot if we wish to see the most discreet and beautiful changes of warm and cold colour within a tonal scheme; and before him to the Dutch landscape painters Ruysdael or Cuyp, and to Rembrandt. After the turn of the century, as Impressionist doctrine spread, the expression 'colour value' came into currency to denote the inclusion of hue in value. Since the degree of warmth or coolness in a colour also affects its relative position in space, value comes to mean the total aspect of a colour in spatial relationship with other colours. A colour will advance or recede as it is changed by being made darker or lighter, warmer or colder, more positive or less positive. In practice, especially applied to visual painting, this means that the colour can be put on in touches, each of which relates spatially to its neighbour, so that the form of a solid is not rounded by modelling from light to dark, but is built up from touches, each of which suggests a measurable distance from the picture plane. We can see in Corot's freer landscapes or Constable's sketches how this is applied with an emphasis on tone and lighting; in Monet's Cathedrals it allows analysis of colour in atmospheric depth; in Cézanne the monumental treatment of solid and space by planes of changing colour. Respect for Poussin has ensured the continuity in French tradition of the principle inherent in the work of all the Old Masters, that space in painting should be continuous, control-

Rothko: 'Reds no 22'

Collection of Mr and Mrs Robert C. Scull

61

Rubens: 'The Fur Coat'

Kunsthistorisches Museum, Vienna

led by forms and colours working together. This derives originally from the attempt of the first Italian realists to create a physically consistent microcosm analogous in its properties to the real and finite physical universe (see page 25). But the older Masters composed on a framework of drawing, building area by area in transparent layers. Velasquez, Rubens, Rembrandt, exploiting the technical possibilities of oil paint towards greater visual frankness, the free handling of volumes, and a more expressive handwriting in which drawing and colour are put in both together, had developed the free brush stroke as a medium for changes of warmer and colder as well as lighter and darker colour, using this means of controlling solid and space in conjunction with conventional tonal modelling. The doctrine of values provided a restatement of this classical doctrine in a way which was convenient for painting direct from the subject in an opaque paste as well as by transparent touches.

Each brush stroke, whether smaller or larger, constitutes a plane parallel to the picture plane, each can in one operation state the sum of local colour and colour conditioned by light; it is even possible to suggest the colour of atmosphere between and in front of objects without glazing (Monet). It allows for the rapidity of execution necessary to painters *en plein air*. It provides a unity of vision and handling; obviates the filled-in outline or the use of tonal modelling as a convention when a flat lighting forbids it. But the danger is that this visual and spatial consistency becomes a substitute for composition; the overall pattern of the painting, especially on the picture plane, gets lost and the grand tradition of design by big divisions and subsidiary divisions, massing of light and dark, precise proportions of areas of colour and linear rhythms, handed down from Byzantium to the Florentines, and from them to Raphael and to Poussin,   dissipated. We can see why Gauguin and later the cubists localized colour and reaffirmed the separating line. While retaining the truth that colour and form are one, they wished to reinstate the composed picture, and the mural grandeur of flat colour. These are the sources from which abstract painters have inherited the control of space by colour used in flat areas parallel to the picture plane.

Cézanne

Cézanne, like the Impressionists, responded to colour and considered the values which reveal formal relationships in space as change of colour rather than change of tone. But he wished to design as the Old Masters did, monumentally in sculptural mass. Although he reproduced the general illumination of southern sunlight with truth and evident enjoyment, he used to long for dull days when the form became clear. There would then be no shadow and he could see the colour as a property of form and not of light. He sought to use his changes of colour as symbols for the continuous movements of forms through space, and not as properties of light. In discussing local colour we saw how the colour changes provided by the lighting condition are the unifying element (while local colour asserts the separateness of objects). On the other hand this unifying light also breaks up the continuity of shape moving into shape by casting shadows and darkening one side of an object so that it is split in two. The grandeur of the form is lost. The early Italians (Piero della Francesca, for example) were dependent for the monumentality which they sought on the tonal modelling suggested by a lighting condition, because their models were in classical sculpture. They solved their problem in a way suited to fresco and tempera, modelling symbolically in very pale tones. In oil paint, later painters developed the play of light and dark as a unifying web which flowed across the composition (chiaroscuro). With Piero, Masaccio, Michelangelo, modelling and colour became properties of form, derived from light but not producing the visual effect of light. Cézanne's temperament and reading of history led him to pursue a similar aim – to do Poussin again from nature. He reduced the differences of tone due to light and produced his volumes by modulations of colour across the form. He retains local colour and tone to a greater or lesser degree according to each visual situation; but across the forms flow the colours, a tendency to blue for turning away from light and for distance, a tendency to orange for turning towards the light and for nearness. The unifying effect of light is represented, but not the light and dark of lit objects. Form is interpreted by colour symbolically. Monumental forms of great subtlety are built in colour from touches of paint, each of which is modified in colour and each of which becomes a plane stating a position in space in relation to every other coloured patch throughout the painting. A tendency to vertical brush strokes affirms that these marks are related to the picture plane and assert the design of the painting on the wall surface. It needs to be restated that it was from nature that Cézanne sought to remake the art of Poussin. Cézanne was a painter of visual sensation and it is the sensation of seeing that he re-creates, not a set formula for rendering form or space. The differences of colour are differences which he has observed. Each piece of the mosaic falls into place in the spatial scheme of

Cézanne: 'Italian Girl Leaning'

Collection of Dr and Mrs Harry Bakwin

the painting within that limited sense of depth which is true to the visual experience of seeing: one thing is behind another, but the eye draws it forward as it looks at it. It is not a conceptual depth, but the sensation of searching the visual field. The Impressionists, even Degas, appear conventional when hung against Cézanne who remains completely the man of this age as well as his own because he takes nothing on trust. He tells us that each man must see afresh from the beginning for himself.

Composition is not simply a convenient framework, nor a necessary but inconvenient means of fitting an idea into a frame. If any device in a painting seems inconvenient it is best to try doing without it. To start with the assertion that there is no such thing as composition may lead to a more necessary order than the inhibiting assertion that everything in a painting must be composed. This then is not an argument for composition in an exclusively classical mould.

The interpenetration of form and meaning is as true of incomplete romantic forms of art as of an exaggerated Gothic characterization of detail. But classical theories of composition do stand for the conscious and deliberate ordering of the means, whereas other points of view embrace to varying degrees an automatic (though not necessarily unconscious) acceptance of intuitions, emotional reactions, gestures and direct sensations. Different kinds of design employ some degree of deliberate formal organization, with an emphasis on one or more of these.

Intuition seems foremost in Chinese and Japanese art; the design is spontaneously written as the sum of contemplative concentration on the subject and its essential meaning. Reality is given a philosophical, not a physical, structure. We marvel at the ability of Chinese and Japanese artists to identify themselves with natural subjects – the sympathy they show for fish or flowers or insects, so that where we would draw the anatomy they draw the essence – as if they knew what it was like to be a fish (without anthropomorphic condescension). By contrast, classical Western art, closely related to work in stone, mosaic or wood, sometimes seems desperately concerned with architectural stability and physical presence.

Expressionism gives us the extreme example of design ordered to emotional demands: the composition is conceived to give the utmost drama and the forms are then pulled this way or that by the psychological forces to which the painter seeks to respond.

The action paintings of Jackson Pollock or early Riopelle show the extreme of gesture; while Impressionism is the type of painting by direct sensation. Action painting and Impressionism are close in spirit.

In the former the organization is read into the painting as it develops (more or less) accidentally. It can be argued that whatever we do automatically must have a deeper essential cause; we ourselves and the accident of our hands become nature, while the extreme Impressionist position is to accept the field of vision exactly as it happens.

Of course the Impressionists themselves took with them to nature conventions which helped them to select (for example, optical perspective and tonal values – no painter starts from scratch), but found new emphases: first the quick impression, and later the analysis of colour, both of which fitted their pantheistic creed of truth to visual sensation. Their acceptance of the whole visual field without rearrangement retrieved composition from the consciously picturesque, just as action painting accepting accident broke the spell of the new picturesque derived from cubism.

Composition in the classical sense is the logical organization of pictorial means. This does not mean that everything we do when we paint must be logical or that our control must necessarily be conscious. We are discussing two things: the logical decisions which we can make consciously or instinctively as a consequence of conscious training, and also the pictorial logic which we can perceive in a completed painting; here we cannot know for certain what was conscious and what was unconscious activity.

The basic ingredients

Restricting ourselves for the moment to design on the flat surface of the canvas, we can assert that a painting consists of several different kinds of interwoven pattern: a scheme of colour, a scheme of light and dark, a system of scale and intervals, an arrangement of shapes, an order of small and large scale patterning, and a network of linear rhythms.

1. Line, shapes, colours

The basic ingredients of a painting are lines, shapes and colours; Delacroix said that composition was 'the organization of analogies'. These must occur not only from contrasts of line, shape and colour, but also from similarities. Very few and simple shapes can produce very complicated designs. The strength of a design is as much in the repeating motifs, the echoes and similarities as in the differences and contrasts.

2. Proportion, interval and scale

An organized use of interval and scale depends on unity of certain proportions which are repeated by similar and different shapes through-

Rembrandt: 'Belshazzar's Feast', detail

National Gallery, London

68

Jackson Pollock: 'No 14 1948'

Collection of Miss Katharine Ordway

out the design; obviously the regularity or irregularity of the various sizes of shapes and the length of interval between similar shapes or lines control the character of the composition fundamentally. Scale also regulates the apparent size of the canvas – whether it seems bigger or smaller than it is, whether the forms are generous or pinched.

3. Contrast of plain and patterning

Contrasted changes of scale can also be seen to control the patterning of some areas and the plainness of others.

The eloquence of Japanese and Chinese paintings often lies in the contrasted and beautifully shaped and proportioned areas of plain background. Not only ornamental patterning (such as a spotted table cloth, foliage or landscape detail) but any small-scale grouping of detail or small objects must be considered as patterning to be played

69

The Master of Luca: Catalan painting of 'The Last Judgment', detail

Archaeological Museum, Diocese of Solsona

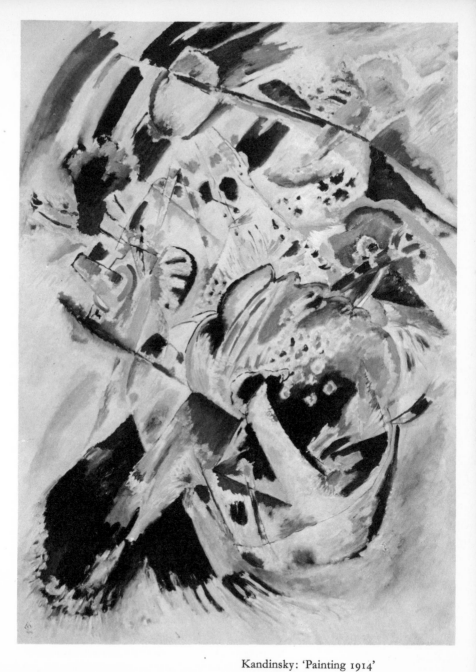

Kandinsky: 'Painting 1914'

The Solomon R. Guggenheim Museum Collection, New York

off against patterning on a larger or smaller scale, or against plainness. The mark of the painter's brush stroke or palette knife also comes in here, or any texture which the painter makes – any mark: close against open, rough against smooth. The painter's brush stroke is indeed another element which can make a separate pattern running through the whole painting with or against the patterns of shape or line or colour.

4. Movement

But just as all sensory experience derives from movement, so we can say that all composition aims at movement. Without movement, there is no life. The movement of the composition is in the varying movement of the parts: the line which carries the eye at greater speed and then slower, the close or separated changes of colour and tone, the slow or fast development of a shape.

I have already said a good deal about line as the sign for movement. For practical purposes we can see the whole movement of a painting as composed from static elements and dynamic; shapes and lines which give repose and stability, and shapes and lines which seem to make motion. Initially it may be said that horizontal and vertical lines are stable. We may think this is so because they echo buildings and structural relationships which we know to be stable, but a truer analogy is with the vertical pull of gravity and the horizontal plane of the earth: the vertical line through our own centre of balance and the ground on which we stand. Diagonals, on the other hand, since they are associated with off-balance, the direction of thrust of energy and friction, are symbols of motion. These things are understood instinctively in terms of our own bodies and simple constructions. The vertical-horizontal axis is of course implied in movement as well as repose. The behaviour of lines, masses and shapes in a painting are analogies of balance, movement, mass and weight and all the other properties of immediate physical experience. But these may also behave in ways which correspond to the motion of gases or molecules or solar systems or magnetic fields – or other less regular patterns of energy.

The repulsions and attractions which occur when we begin to make marks on a sheet of paper provide an interesting explanation of how movement begins on a canvas (I refer to *Basic Design* in this series, and the theories of Arnheim). A mark between two others will appear to be attracted to the nearest, a mark near to the edge of the picture will be attracted to it, a mark on a line will either be in the centre and pulled equally to one end or the other, or the nearer it is to one end the more

Mondrian: 'Composition, with red, yellow and blue, 1930'

Collection of Alfred Roth, Zurich

it will be pulled towards that end. If we make a map of the attractions and counter-attractions which operate in a rectangle, it will appear rather like a map of a magnetic field – the big pull to the centre, the pull to each side, with a special pull to the centre of each side and a big pull to each corner. When we put a number of marks within this field we can discover special positions which produce equilibrium more subtle than positions which are obviously symmetrical. The sides of a square or rectangle are also pulled by the marks which we make. By strong lines we can literally (to the point of optical illusion) pull a rectangle out of shape. It can be made to look much longer or squarer or quite cock-eyed.

This way of considering movement on a canvas appears attractive because of its optical and perceptual approach, but how much is optical and how much suggestion is difficult to say. If we draw a dot in the centre of a square and a dot near the edge in the middle of the right-hand side and think in magnetic terms, the right-hand dot is obviously being attracted by the right-hand side because it is nearest to it; but if we think in terms of a centrifugal force, obviously the centre dot wishes to stay in the middle but the right-hand one is being stopped (not attracted) by the edge (we do not want it to 'go off'). On the other hand, if we think of the two dots as linked in movement (one-way traffic) they are both anxious to move off into the empty space on the left. If we then remove the centre spot, surely the right-hand spot by itself would like to invade all that empty space to the left? It will indeed if we imagine it to be a goldfish, or even without being so specific elongate its shape a little. If we imagine our marks to be cars (circulating), or billiard balls (cannoning) or balloons (floating), or moons (circling) or dogs (fighting) they will appear to suffer from different forces or attractions. Surely all that is really being said is that if something is very close to something else it appears to be related, that if there is a space it is possible to fill it, that symmetry is more static than asymmetry, that if we draw a line it suggests a barrier, that a corner is really a pocket, and so on. All of which suggests a language of symbol and analogy. A V sign pointing to the left suggests an arrow moving to the left; but if we call it a symbol for a radiating light, it instantly suggests movement in the opposite direction. If it is a symbol for a hinge or a crocodile's jaws, the movement seems vertical. It does not really matter if the hen produced the egg or vice versa. But it does seem that analogies and psychological suggestions are as powerful and fundamental as perceptual (psychophysical) factors in art and as yet indistinguishable from them. It is very difficult to avoid the conclusion that formal values in art have no meaning until they become signs for some intelligible process. Form is not significant until it signifies something.

Space

So far we have only considered the organization of a painting in two dimensions – as a flat pattern on the surface of the canvas. Now we must consider composition in depth.

The difference between a flat painting and painting in depth is a matter of degree. There is always a design on the surface, always some degree of suggested depth (or projection). There is no question of one kind of painting which is flat, and another in depth. From the very first mark made on paper a symbolic relationship of object to background is begun, and from the first patch of colour a sensation of space.

Space by colour

Flat colours laid one against the other produce the sensation of space

74

which we call 'movement of colour'. Directly we place different colours and tones side by side we have a sensation of planes in depth parallel to the picture plane (picture surface). To a contemporary painter there is special virtue in the use of colour to suggest space; colour seems the most natural and economical way of controlling volume; and because it appears to produce an actual sensation of space, while space produced by means of drawing appears contrived and mechanical, colour is therefore considered a legitimate way of representing relationships of space, while modelling by tone, planes and other conceptual means such as perspective and foreshortening are suspect. But I do not think this distinction can be made. The changes of colour in a painting which appear to advance or recede are not produced in the same way as the sensations which indicate distance to my eye: in painting simple changes of chemical substance are used to represent alterations of frequency and quantity of light which have been produced in infinitely more complicated and varied ways.

The sensation of colour advancing and receding in relation to the picture plane is as much a symbolic sign language, when used systematically to indicate pictorial depth, as modelling or planes. But the reason why colour seems to give a true sensation of space lies in the fact that it is a physical link between the observed reality and the means of representation. The actual properties of pigment – texture, consistency and colour – provide a tangible bridge to the visual world. For colour in a painting (to whatever symbolic end it is used) is also real, whereas shape and space on a flat surface can only be signified.

Colour provides a sure way of controlling space while making sure that the picture plane (the surface of the wall or the canvas or the page) is never forgotten. When used in conjunction with the symbolic representation of three-dimensional solids, it is the only way of making sure that the shapes and the colour tie together in a series of consistent spatial relationships. But because our sources of information are tactile (form) as well as visual (colour), colour and drawing must be used together to make a consistent pictorial structure. If we suddenly modelled up a flat primitive, a Russian ikon or a Persian or Byzantine painting in which local colour is used to separate and distinguish objects as flat planes, the inconsistency would produce an incredibly vulgar result. This would be because the modelled form might suggest solids, but the flat bright local colour would not be gradated to make the space in which the solid could exist. The discreet atmospheric colour of Piero della Francesca or Masaccio should be pondered. It is the sensibility of colour to space in its own right which makes it possible to model forms; and the practice of modelling must start from a knowledge of relationships of coloured surfaces and not from the colouring up of modelled forms. Just as a sense of mass precedes line, we now see that colour precedes mass. This is not to say that it need necessarily do so in practice – but it must do so in technical understanding. In nature the mass exists: the line is imagined. In painting the colour exists: the mass is inferred. The common belief of beginners that tonal contrast and tonal dilution alone can usually be used to indicate space may seem closest to purely visual experience; but this does not accord with the mural principle of pictorial construction that positive contrasts and strengths of colour and tone must be maintained across the whole surface of the painting.

Space from shape

Just as from the very beginning our flat pattern is disturbed by sensations of depth provided by colours, so lines and the contours of flat shapes spontaneously suggest solid shapes or planes moving into the picture space. A spiral, a zigzag line or shapes which overlap are simple examples. A rhomboid appears as a receding rectangle; recession is strongly suggested by repeating shapes which become progressively smaller. It is only a matter of degree from these to the silhouette of a foreshortened human figure or a simple system of linear perspective. Modelling, used since the earliest cave drawings, is not different in kind. It is just as legitimate a way of suggesting space as colour or contour or planes or diminishing scale. But overmodelling which destroys the consistency of space – contradicting the colour relationships and destroying the interlocking of planes – is another matter. The modulation of form by changes of colour rather than changes of tone is the modern and subtler version of this means of describing spatial relationships, explored by Cézanne, and in keeping with the urge to prevent drawing and colour becoming separate activities.

There seems to be a strong impression that certain representational means are more respectable than others. Many of us are confused by the word illusion, which has different shades of meaning. It can mean an optical illusion; it can also mean the imaginative co-operation between artist and spectator which all art demands. Modelled forms or linear perspectives, or Cézanne's use of colour to correspond to changing planes, are not illusions in the narrow sense but kinds of (symbolic) representation; a street painted in perspective does not provide the illusion that it is a real street but merely shows what a

Matisse: 'The Painter's Studio'

Pushkin Museum, Moscow
© *S. P. A. D. E. M., Paris, 1965*

street looks like. If it is well painted we may be invited to imagine what it is like to walk in the street; the strength of the sensation is in the imagination. An artist's skill lies in his power to stimulate the imagination and to suggest. Only in a limited field of still-life or in the theatre with controlled lighting can painting sometimes take on the optical illusion of reality – and that only rarely when a repetitive perspective such as arcading is used. The only recorded case of a painter walking into his own painting was the Chinese artist Wu Taotsz (eighth century A. D.) who shut a painted door behind him and was never seen again.

The picture plane

All the shapes and lines and colours in a painting have therefore a twofold role, in depth and on the surface of the canvas. (The rhomboid on the surface is the tilted rectangle in depth.) A painting is not fulfilled unless the composition is performing both these functions. This fundamental double meaning of each ingredient is the machinery by which analogies that give meaning at different levels of experience are produced.

There is nothing mysterious in the modern emphasis on flat painting; it is a matter of common sense. Painting is first of all organization on a flat surface – that is factually all that painting is. The painter who does not continue to respect the flat organization as he elaborates visual detail has lost control: there will be no colour scheme, no relationships of scale, no rhythmic contrasts of shape and line, no possibility of a coherent image. Although in figurative painting we take it for granted and may be unaware that it is so, we see the flat before we see the depth because we must see what actually exists before we see what is suggested.

But immediately we see the surface pattern we also unavoidably receive the sensation of depth – from both colours and shapes. A design which ignores depth is as full of contradictions as a design which ignores surface. Directly there is depth there is a correspondence to both visual and tactile experience. But representation whether of specific objects or abstract properties is not in fact but by suggestion. Space can only be suggested, not made. The surface organization and the organization of volumes are not incompatible but complementary, part and parcel of the same act of composing and, if there is to be unity, must be controlled together.

The richness of different kinds of painting as a means of communication has come from the elaboration of abstract signs which correspond to the properties, objects and situations of sense experience, images developed from them and meanings given to them. There is nothing intrinsically unpainterly about highly naturalistic or descriptive painting unless the means of representation begin to destroy the coherent articulation of the surface design. This is the difference between Rembrandt and Rembrandtesque, Vermeer and mock Dutch.

The important thing is that space can only be suggested, not realized, and that there are different means of representing space but we cannot use them all at full pressure – tone and colour, modelling and planes. If we use a language of economical signs, tender gradations and shallow space we can unfold a whole universe on the canvas.

The volumes which occur in painting are either the result of differences in colour (including tone) or of drawing (linear or modelled geometry and changes of scale) or a combination of these. But in any case depth is in relation to the picture plane and corresponds to our own physical sensation of space obtained by sight and touch. This is the basis of the symbolism of space. But we must avoid the academic absurdity of imagining that form in painting corresponds to some sort of static Euclidean structure, which has an actual physical existence.

Obviously different painters and different ages have structured reality differently. Egyptian, Byzantine, Chinese and Renaissance art each have different points of view in which various physical and psychological considerations play their part; we see quite different perspectives. The narrative processional and cyclic qualities of Egyptian art are quite different from the Euclidean constructions and sculptural symbols of the Renaissance, or the hierarchical theological structure of Byzantine iconography. No painters have been exclusively preoccupied with physical structure for its own sake. In all painting emphasis of colour or scale or distortions of shape occur for quite other reasons. The perfect rendering of a theoretical physical structure would be without life. In any case our own sense of physical structure has been geared by relativity and modern physics to movement and energy. Our need to represent physical structure at all is cancelled by psychoanalysis; this is reflected in our painting.

Otto Demus explains the three-quarter face in Byzantine mosaics by the necessity of each holy figure to communicate with the congregation as the object of their veneration, and at the same time with the other actors in the sacred drama across the space contained by the curved niche. So Christ's story might be convincingly told. In the same way we can interpret the perpetual profile of Egyptian art as due

Gold from Nubia, *c* 1400 B.C.

British Museum, London

to the need to prevent the spectator from interfering with a cycle of events which was designed to accompany the dead king for ever. Shut in a tomb, the paintings are not intended to involve the spectator at all but to exist in their own right. A figure full-face is a figure inviting worship or adoration; a figure in profile goes about its own business. Depth draws the spectator into the painting and involves him in the issue. The flat surface of Egyptian art keeps the image aloof and intact. Events are portrayed realistically and graphically as a narrative written on the surface of the wall and designed in relation to the actual writing which completed the picture. By contrast Byzantine art presents a liturgical drama which involves the spectator: Renaissance art almost invites physical participation.

Such differences depend on different ways of looking at reality. But the formal means by which depth can be rendered are basically the same, summed up by the conventional theory of the picture plane and the picture space projected consistently behind (or in front). Whatever measures are taken to assert depth, corresponding measures must be taken to reaffirm the wall surface. The image must be consistently flat or consistent in depth.

Perspective

By perspective we generally mean the deliberate control of space in a painting. Linear perspective is control by drawing. Often we talk of perspective as the optical system explored by Italian painters which in one variation or another became the convention normal to European art. It is important to recall that this system was never until the nineteenth century just a way of representing appearances, but always a method of composing a painting, never used alone but in combination with other mathematical theories of design. But there are many kinds of perspective. Every painting has a perspective of some sort. The first and most important function of a perspective is to establish the position of the spectator in relation to the painting (by the position in which he establishes himself and also therefore the spectator, the painter states his attitude to the image which he creates). The viewpoint establishes the point of view. In our Russian ikon, for instance, we have seen (page 23) how St George rides on high, admired and venerated, looking down on evil. The ikon is designed to this end. Or we can see how Brueghel takes a high viewpoint, the whole world laid out map-like at our feet, to discuss the multiplicity of human activities on the familiar mystery of the earth. It is clear that horizontal divisions or an implied eye-level are extremely important – the basic landscape choice of how much land to how much sky is fundamental. We can imagine different painters standing on a bare plain: one draws a straight horizontal line and paints so much land, so much sky; another all sky; another only the earth at his feet; another a circle representing the world bounded by a circular horizon as he turns round. Each establishes an attitude. Some paintings use more than one eye-level, directing the spectator's attention in a way which corresponds to an upward or downward movement of his head. Others use multiple viewpoints at a fixed level. We travel along the picture. Others have no fixed viewpoint, as if every part of the elevation were of equal importance. Recently we have seen paintings which achieve an optical effect as the spectator walks past. By the perspective suggested the painter invites us to view his creation in a certain way. He contrives the degree to which we enter into the painting or remain as detached spectators. The perspective controls the degree and kind of self-identification which the painting offers. Italian optical perspective with a fixed viewpoint was welcomed in its origin as a method of achieving physical unity. But it is also easy to see why we should have become impatient with the rigidity of convention set by a fixed view-

Brueghel: 'The Hunters in the Snow (January)'

Kunsthistorisches Museum, Vienna

point. We spend our lives in motion; we are conscious of the relativity rather than the permanence of visual experience.

Planes

Both the sculptural intention of Byzantine composition and the Euclidean structure of conventional Italian perspective have given the concept of the plane great importance in Western painting. The plane has become the painter's own symbolic geometry. This tradition we inherit especially through Poussin, David, Cézanne and the cubists. Planes remain in a large area of abstract art the chief unit of design and the symbol for determinate relationships in space. Where the convention of a fixed viewpoint in relation to nature is abandoned, the manipulation of flat planes remains (in Braque or Matisse, for instance) as the method of continuing relationships throughout the painting and firmly tying depth to surface design. The weakness of the academic tradition in England is largely due to planes being seen only as a piecemeal method of analysing nature (for example, as an aid to the accurate drawing of a head). In fact planes have a doubtful value as a way of observing individual structures, since it is sections which matter and not surface. The flattening of a rounded surface into arbitrary facets leads to falsification. But planes are a valid conventional (symbolic) equivalent on the flat to volumes in depth and the only solid method of pictorial construction. Colour alone will not produce the sensation of solid matter, nor line, unless the contour indicates changes of plane.

The old old story of the student who cannot get the ground to lie down is due to his confused thinking. His reasons for wanting the ground to lie down are suspect. The 'ground' is only one of several horizontal planes which are parallel to each other. There will also be vertical planes which enter the picture diagonally at different angles and there may be others parallel to the picture plane. The ground plane is no more important than any other planes small or large. If the painting is composed on a valid system of perspective (not necessarily Italian) with all planes equally considered and strongly related, the ground will lie down; if the painting is not composed on some such system then it does not matter in the least whether the ground lies down or not. The plane is not an intermittent means of dealing with trouble spots in a painting; it is a formal invention for manipulating the volumes.

The painter must make his planes and place his planes as he wishes them to be. Even if he is deriving his planes by direct observation, the plane read into nature is not the same thing as the formal synthesis which he must make on the canvas. As with tone or colour he must make explicit what is only implicit in nature, and choose between conflicting alternative interpretations.

The great hidden strength of Picasso, Matisse, Braque, Vuillard, Bonnard, Modigliani and the other twentieth-century painters of the school of Paris, as of their forerunners Le Nain, Latour, David, Millet, Old Papa Corot and all, has lain in the clarity and logic with which they manipulated planes (hidden, that is, to the Englishman bred in a foggier, Poussin-less tradition). There must be something very odd in our climate that we praise Stubbs only for his tenacity in dissecting horses and rate Zoffany as just another portrait painter with an embarrassing foreign accent. Constable and Turner we admire not

Brueghel: detail. The strange shapes combined from these hounds (like the forms in a Miró) show the means by which our imaginations are stirred

Kunsthistorisches Museum, Vienna

Picasso: 'Three Musicians', 1921

Museum of Modern Art, New York. Mrs Simon Guggenheim Fund.
© *S. P. A. D. E. M., Paris, 1965*

because but in spite of their ability to construct. We recognize Sickert's technical acumen but we fail to see the logic behind his witty and eccentric touch. Moreover when we do pay academic lip-service to planes we think of a static architectural framework and not of the interplay of coloured surfaces which gives movement and life to a canvas in the perpetual antithesis of depth to picture plane.

It may seem that a related flat design (as in primitive ikons or Egyptian wall painting or an abstract painting where every plane is parallel to the picture plane) provides the surest means of producing a coherent painting as well as the strongest appeal to our emotions. Perhaps this is the moment to restate the great advantages of making full use of the picture space in depth as well as the picture surface. Most important of all:

1. It enlarges the area to be filled; ikons, Byzantine mosaics and, in spite of most carefully and beautifully calculated spaces, Egyptian decorations appear crowded compared to the great Italian naturalists. A modern abstract painting retains dignity of spacing as long as the ingredients are very simple. But by opening out the picture space in

84

depth the great Italians were able to retain the magnificence of heavy monumental forms, to use at one time a great many figures, architectural motifs and landscape detail, and to make complicated patterns with great simplicity (echoing one rhythmic theme within another by changes of scale). They could do this without any crowding or confusion because there is a consistent system of depth.

2. Because the eye adjusts itself to changes in scale which are justified by formal perspective, the proportions throughout the painting remain adjusted to the scale of the human body. Instead of the thing which is smaller becoming less important it can retain equal or even greater psychological importance than larger masses. Because the eye moves into the picture to read events in depth, the scale of shapes on the picture plane is played off against the real scale of objects interpreted in perspective; far subtler analogies of shape can be achieved and orchestrations of form which are highly complicated yet simplified and grand. In depth scale can be used to its fullest advantage. Similarly in Brueghel or Patinir we see the use of plastic signs to organize a microcosm of beehive activity without any loss of simplicity.

Nicolas Poussin: 'Landscape with a Snake'

National Gallery, London

Plastic analogies

Directly we see the shapes on the canvas take on spatial properties and represent something, the abstract repetition of shapes and proportions and patterns in the scheme of the painting takes on a new power. That of the magician. The same shape repeated in different objects, in trees, in rock, or water or sky, or in the shapes of human beings or animals, and in negative shapes left between, in reverse, on the same scale or on a different scale, not only provides a melodic theme but also (like rhymes, alliteration and assonance in literature) poetic links which make associations and affinities between objects and events and areas of the painting, or point dramatic contrasts. These metaphorical links may be between patterned areas and plain or modelled solids echoed by flat shapes, or between parallel lines of which one moves into the picture and one across the surface; in this way the movement of landscape continues the movement of figures, or the inanimate objects in an interior make their personalities felt. The formal link is also *always a psychological link*.

It is here perhaps that we should talk of ambiguity: first of all, the obvious way in which shapes and colours can be read in alternative ways, and then the less obvious allusions by which a form which quite obviously represents one thing also calls to mind a variety of other things – by its own shape or the shape which it makes where it joins another, or the way in which it echoes some other part of the canvas. These are the formal devices by which a painting which appears to be about one thing carries a far different message – and not necessarily one message but many; the landscape which is the human body, the still life which is the city, the human body which is the temple, rocks which are clowns and tragic vegetation. The simile and the metaphor are as much a part of painting as they are of speech. Analogy is the means of extending human understanding.

Division of space

The problem of composition is to keep the eye moving but to prevent it moving too fast, to give it time to browse but not to get bored. The eye must be invited to each area of the painting, offered some interest and then moved on. A painting is not read like a book: the eye must be persuaded to go on looking at the same areas over and over again, but in a different order, finding new connexions: the meaning unfolds as new relationships are discovered. Centres of interest make fixed points of reference for the eye to return to each time it has made a journey. Divisions (lines where dark meets light or colour changes) circumscribe the areas which the eye is to examine for a while. Passages allow the eye to move through from one area or one form to another. (By passages we mean similarity of tone or colour and gradations of tone or colour which prevent a form from being completely enclosed.)

Most paintings have certain major divisions, vertical or horizontal, caused by lines (visible or *implied*) which run right across the canvas. Where to place these divisions or allow them to occur is the first problem in the logical development of a pictorial organization.

Vertical divisions

If we divide a sheet of paper once, unequally, with a vertical line and place a mark on each side of this line where it seems most fitting, we have the basis of this type of compositional scheme. We have divided the picture space into two unequal parts and placed a centre of interest in each. If we take a fairly detailed photograph and draw a similar line through, in each unequal half some feature will take on prominence as a centre of interest. After the first unequal division the pattern of asymmetrical balance must be followed through consistently as further partitions are made. But in elaborate organizations, an unobtrusive reminder of the symmetry implied within the balance is usually given. Very often this takes the form of an object which marks the vertical centre line or a subtly implied line through the horizontal centre line. The purpose is obvious; to assert the hidden symmetry required by balance. This is done by apparently instinctive painters. Van Gogh out of doors almost invariably marks the centre or near centre of his canvas. In classical figure compositions the sense of suspended movement is often achieved on a central axis.

Symmetrical divisions

Symmetrical compositions are characteristic of traditional religious iconography. Symmetrical designs have a powerful ritualistic significance; symmetry is very memorable and therefore reserved for impressive, extraordinary and theologically important events: the Crucifixion, the Ascension, the Trinity. But symmetry is also used in designs for crafts because it is easier to remember (carpets, carvings, ceramics) and because it fits in with the symmetry of pottery, furniture and architecture. The genesis of the ritual importance of symmetrical signs, and therefore of symmetry, in religious art lies in primitive magic. Compositionally, symmetry throws into relief those details which are dissimilar. Combined vertical and horizontal symmetry has been rare.

'Virgin Orans', Yoroslavl School, *c.* 1220 *Tretyakov Gallery, Moscow*

The causes of a renewed interest in symmetrical composition among abstract painters include a present need to test and contradict the half truths of traditional practice, enquiry into the basis of both perception and design, desire to assert a contemporary style which can exert an environmental influence through architecture and applied arts, and perhaps a little the sense of the potency of a magical presentation. In a Crucifixion the fact that a figure marks the central division means that there is a main interest in the centre of the canvas. Symmetry with two objects and a central space or division is not uncommon but presents much greater difficulties.

Horizontal divisions

Vertical divisions allude to architectural themes, horizontal divisions to landscape. In many paintings there is an implied horizontal which is the horizon line – or an obvious meeting of sky and ground or ground and foliage (mountains, hillside). In landscape this is often the obvious major division – the first decision to be made in still life, the meeting of a horizontal and vertical plane.

It will be seen that the major planes in Western painting have usually been used like screens or flats in the theatre. This is the simplest and most obvious symbol for space: two flat planes which overlap. Our Russian St George, for example, has one plane for the horse and St George, and behind a plane for the hills, and behind that a plane for the sky. Events within each flat screen are rigorously controlled to remain there. Each retains its difference of tone and colour. This economical way of suggesting space stays throughout European painting; with the development of naturalism we find these flat screens disguised by subtlety of modelling and the depth within each extended by tonal gradations; also the edges are softened by atmospheric passages. But this system of overlapping remains the basic method of suggesting depth without actually making it by slavish imitation of changes of tone and colour. There is no need for tonal dilution. André L'Hôte describes this very well as a 'false staircase' – far things are as close as near things in the sense that they are just as strongly painted. Space can be achieved without punching holes in the surface of the canvas. Where vertical divisions tend to produce the sense that we are moving into different rooms – they separate one part of the picture from another, making smaller pictures within larger ones with their own centres of interest – horizontal divisions do not usually make such strong barriers; they are hurdles over which the eye travels, holding the eye for long enough to explore each layer and enhance the sense of depth.

Diagonal divisions

Diagonals are the natural leads which take the eye into a painting. This may take the form of linear arabesques or contour lines which establish diagonal planes, or foreshortened volumes which move into the picture space. There are many examples (Vermeer, cubism, Tintoretto) of the deliberate use of diagonal planes leading into the picture space (dynamic planes) contrasted with planes which lie parallel to the picture plane (static planes). This in itself becomes a system of composition in which different rates of movement, as well as movement in different directions, within the picture space complement each other. In this equilibrium of movement not all planes are explicit, but may be invisible planes contained in space between points or contours or objects. Vermeer builds his composition by a musical arrangement of visible and *implied* rectangles of varying scale, some parallel to the picture plane, others projected in depth.

In European art the movement of diagonals and diagonal planes are traditionally held in suspension by the verticals and horizontals which give architectural stability. But parallel diagonals are also used. Sometimes a diagonal is used as a major division. In oriental art isometric perspective and a generalized high viewpoint lend themselves to the possibility of composition entirely by diagonals. The parallel lines of the perspective provide orderly diagonal movement, and a balance of points where lines reach the edge of the picture on each side. The convention of (to our eyes) reverse perspective, when the parallelogram as it recedes appears to widen, is used intermittently both to slow down movement into the picture space and to prevent the surface of the panel from losing its importance. This 'reverse' perspective is not contrary to visual experience: if we place ourselves three or four feet away from the *corner* of a table or a rug and two or three feet above it, we will have the illusion that the end farthest from us is wider than the end nearest to us, which appears more foreshortened because we are almost looking down it. (To our astonishment, this can even be verified by a measuring rod held at arm's length.) But of course our Chinese or Japanese artist is concerned not with verisimilitude but with design. Such diagonal compositions take their place very naturally on Japanese screens, where the diagonal lines echo the planes of the folded panels. The picture surface itself, folded in three, consists of three diagonal planes; there cannot be any true horizontal, and a Western perspective in depth would produce a series of conflicting viewpoints. The only rational solution is a perspective of parallel diagonals. This is an excellent example of how each art form gets its own laws, and shows how rash it is to attribute unfamiliar conventions to inability.

In Oriental art and less often in Western art we find a major division of the panel is diagonal.

Where the speed of a diagonal line reaching the edge of the canvas tends to take the eye off the panel, a return line is often used to take the eye back into the picture; but this is usually implied rather than aggressively stated.

These obvious ways of dividing the picture space correspond to three traditional modes of composition (in describing these I am indebted to André L'Hôte).

1. The static architectural compositions beloved by the great mathematicians. Partition is by vertical and horizontal divisions. Diagonal movements and animated centres of interest occur within the ordered spaces provided by this framework as if in the rooms of a mansion. The sparing use of curves and diagonals, the circle or isosceles triangle take on intense but dignified dramatic significance against vertical and horizontal. This is the order of the classical cultures of Greece, Byzantium and the early Renaissance, and also of the Protestant ethic of Vermeer and Mondrian. Whether by design or intuition the proportions of such compositions must correspond to mathematical laws whose principles we see consciously employed by Piero, Vermeer and Seurat. This is the composition of space, of domestic order or of philosophical enquiry.

2. Divisions are still by straight lines, often through the axis of forms. But within the areas partitioned, diagonal lines dominate and the composition is no longer static. Triangles, parallelograms or Maltese crosses achieve an equilibrium of movement more or less momentary in feeling according to the degree of asymmetry. Weight and balance and the recurrent physical sensations or activities of the human body are suggested. This is the type of composition which engages movement, balance, mass and weight. There is a demand for the spectator to identify his own sensations of weight, his balance and movement with those in the painting. This is composition of ordered movement.

3. Curvilinear compositions in which opposed circular or oval concentric movements or eccentric curved movements dominate the design. Extreme relativity of movement is demonstrated by spiral convolutions which restlessly explore the picture space in depth, and offer strong analogies to natural forces or psychological conditions

Giovanni Bellini: 'Young
woman at her toilet'.
Surreal analogies

Kunsthistorisches Museum, Vienna

Saenredam: 'Church of
S. Bavo, Haarlem'. An
abstract vision

National Gallery, London

beyond human control; this is the composition of energy. Identification is with growth.

Tintoretto shows the classical version where the curves are based on mathematically determined arcs. In works by Rubens (especially in certain landscapes), El Greco, Turner and later Van Gogh, we find spontaneous and intuitive variations. Delacroix is subject to rule of numbers and also spontaneous eruption, while Impressionist and Expressionist painters bring this kind of organization into our century.

This is the composition of energy. Identification is with the forces which seem to defy gravity – winds, tides, the record of volcanic upheaval left in rock, growth, fermentation, the motions of heavenly bodies and atomic structures, the muscle rather than bone, the light which dissolves while it reveals, the hidden turmoils of the mind. We find at one end of the scale a correspondence to the ordered irregularity of nature, at the other that decomposition which fascinated the romantics and still fascinates our own age – the invocations of chaos.

Of course such divisions are generalized and arbitrary; each can be subdivided again; painters have painted in one mode and then another, or mixed them. But they demonstrate the precise correspondence of formal means to mental attitude – of style to meaning. It is for each painter to re-invent the means which suit his purpose.

The rule of numbers

We know that Piero della Francesca and Uccello, to mention the most obvious among the Italians, or Vermeer among northern painters, were most passionate mathematicians, that Delacroix used mathematical systems and Seurat was inspired by this study. The cubists at least flirted with the golden section, which most of the Old Masters and many other moderns have used as a rule of thumb. Picasso, for instance, adhered to the grand tradition in starting with a framework of guiding lines on which to place the divisions of space, the directions of movement, the axes of forms and the geometrical patterns to which they should conform, but making evident in an arbitrary way the system which the Old Masters concealed.

It is among the painters who used these linear traces that the golden section found its conscious adherents. This proportion is described by the division of a line in such a way that the larger part is to the smaller as the whole to the larger, or the series $1 - 2 - 3 - 5 - 8 - 13 - 21 - 34 - 55 - 89 - 144$, etc.; as the numbers advance they approach the golden section. Much has been written on this subject and many

Rubens: 'Philemon and Baucis'

Kunsthistorisches Museum, Vienna

investigations made to prove the frequency of these and other favoured proportions in natural growth, in Greek architecture and in the intuitive choices made by the eye. We can remember that historically mathematics developed from the study of the stars for religious and magical reasons as well as for the primitive needs of building, irrigation and surveying. Numbers have always been given mystical and symbolic significance, and for this reason we may suspect the mathematical approach. But a commonsense view suggests that the eye demands and the mind is satisfied by a balance which can be perceived but which has a cause which is not immediately obvious: the golden

Turner: 'Steamer in a Snowstorm'

National Gallery, London

section satisfies this demand. Those of us who feel that such mathematical traces would be a straitjacket can take comfort in the fact that as many bad artists have sought the rule of numbers as good ones. But few of us who hope that intuition will carry us through can avoid the sneaking desire to know a great deal more about it without involving ourselves in years of fruitless research. If science has made the old rules unacceptable, perhaps it is time for a reappraisal by a modern mathematician in relation to the growing body of theoretical knowledge of perception. If harmony, discord, assonance, dissonance, symmetry, scale, balance, proportion mean anything it is in relation to mathematical series.

p31 — *apprehension* acquired in art as in reading

Acknowledgements

for supplying photographs of paintings illustrated in
this book or for giving permission to reproduce copy-
right material, the author and publishers acknowledge
with gratitude the following:
Galerie Charpentier, Paris (p 2)
Basic Books Inc., New York (p 6)
Signal, London (p 7)
Kasmin Gallery (p 8)
The Trustees of the National Gallery, London
              (pp 16, 17, 24, 43, 49, 68, 85, 92, 98)
The Trustees of the British Museum (pp 27, 80)
Ark Magazine (p 31)
The Arts Council of Great Britain (pp 39, 47, 55, 65, 71, 84)
The Trustees of the Chatsworth Settlement (p 36)
Marlborough Fine Art Ltd, London (pp 61, 69)
Messrs Thames and Hudson, London (pp 69, 73)
Other acknowledgements are made beneath the illustrations.